POINTS, PITHOUSES, AND PIONEERS

POINTS, PITHOUSES, AND PIONEERS

Tracing Durango's Archaeological Past

Philip Duke and Gary Matlock

University Press of Colorado

Copyright © 1999 by the University Press of Colorado

Published by the University Press of Colorado
P.O. Box 849
Niwot, Colorado 80544

The University Press of Colorado is a cooperative publishing enterprise supported, in part, by Adams State College, Colorado State University, Fort Lewis College, Mesa State College, Metropolitan State College of Denver, University of Colorado, University of Northern Colorado, University of Southern Colorado, and Western State College of Colorado.

The paper used in this publication meets the minimum requirements of the American National Standard for Information Sciences—Permanence of Paper for Printed Library Materials. ANSI Z39.48–1984

Library of Congress Cataloging-in-Publication Data
Duke, P. G.
    Points, pithouses, and pioneers : tracing Durango's archaeological
past / Philip Duke, Gary Matlock.
        p.   cm.
    Includes bibliographical references (p.   ).
    ISBN 0-87081-519-9 (alk. paper). — 0-87081-556-3 (pbk. : alk. paper).
    1. Durango Region (Colo.)—Antiquities.   2. Excavations
(Archaeology)—Colorado—Durango Region.   3. Archaeology—Colorado—
Durango Region.   I. Matlock, Gary, 1941–   . II. Title.
F784.D9D85   1999
978.8'29—dc21   99-41475
                                                                        CIP

08 07 06 05 04 03 02 01 00 99   10 9 8 7 6 5 4 3 2 1

Contents

Contents

Figures

Figures

Acknowledgments

Our thanks to Catherine Conrad and Todd Ellison, of the Center of Southwest Studies at Fort Lewis College, for helping us track down local photographs and archival material. Thanks also to Liz Bauer of Mesa Verde National Park, Jeff Dean of the Laboratory of Tree-Ring Research, the staff of the Arizona State Museum, and Robert McDaniel of the Animas Museum for helping us locate archival information and photographs in their respective institutions. Dean Saitta and Bob York reviewed the manuscript, and their comments immeasurably improved the final version. We appreciate the information provided to us by Morley Ballantine, Susan Davies, Tim LaFrance, Leo Lloyd, John Sanders, Duane Smith, Noreen Smith, and Jill Tripp. Steve Dye and Beau Shriever did the photography and maps, without which this book would have been incomplete. Rodney Cross very kindly flew us over Durango to get the aerial shots. We also wish to acknowledge John Ware, Steve Fuller, Francis Smiley, and Florence Lister, whose synthetic studies in and around Durango have done so much to clarify the nature of Ancestral Pueblo occupation in the area. Philip Duke would like to thank Jamie Karlson for teaching him so much about Southwestern archaeology so many years ago and Doug Scott for so graciously welcoming him to the area. We owe a special debt of gratitude to Mona Charles for providing us with information on her ongoing work. We also thank Joan Sherman for her excellent copyediting skills and we are especially grateful to Laura Furney, our editor at UPC, for all her good

Acknowledgments

counsel and willingness to accommodate our numerous vagaries. Finally, we acknowledge the tremendous work of all the amateur and avocational archaeologists who, over the years, have made the study of Durango's past such an enjoyable and stimulating exercise for us.

Points, Pithouses, and Pioneers

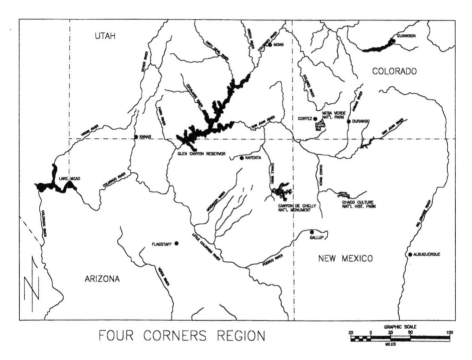

FOUR CORNERS REGION

1.1 Four Corners region, showing location of Durango and major Anasazi (Ancestral Pueblo) sites of Mesa Verde, Chaco Canyon, and Canyon de Chelly.

1
Introduction

Durango, a picturesque little town with some 14,000 residents, is about
an hour's drive from Mesa Verde and just over two hours from Chaco
Canyon, two widely known and well-studied archaeological sites (Figure 1.1). Yet the town itself doesn't have a single standing archaeological ruin within its boundaries. Why, then, would we choose to
write a book on Durango archaeology, especially since there are
literally dozens of books on Southwest archaeology currently on the
market?

Actually, we chose this locale for several compelling reasons. Archaeologists have long considered Durango and the Animas River
valley to be among the most important locations for our understanding of the prehistory of the American Southwest. The Animas valley
was home to a large prehistoric population that lived several centuries
earlier than that at much better known archaeological sites such as
Mesa Verde and Chaco Canyon. Moreover, Durango's location at the
boundary between the Rocky Mountains and the desert offers archaeologists the opportunity to investigate how ancient populations lived
in a "marginal" environment.

Yet, despite the importance of Durango's archaeology, no synthesis of all the work conducted in this area has been made available to
either professionals or the general public. Since the mid-1990s, professional archaeologists, among them Steve Fuller and Francis Smiley,
have produced some excellent monographs on Durango, but these were
written primarily for colleagues in the field. Similarly, Florence Lister

recently published a first-class book on Durango archaeology, but it concentrates on the Anasazi (especially those of the Falls Creek area) and on the often acrimonious relationships between professional and amateur archaeologists in Durango during the 1930s and 1940s. We hope that our book can supplement these and other excellent studies by providing a concise review for the general reader of *all* of Durango's past, while at the same time describing what contemporary archaeologists do and what they have the *potential* to do, not just in Durango itself but elsewhere as well.

Just as important, we hope the reader will see that the story of Durango's archaeological past is a case study of how the public can become actively involved in the practice of archaeology. In fact, Durango's archaeological story is an excellent example for other communities across the nation because residents of the town, which has always been a starting point for travelers, tourists, and archaeologists in the Southwest, have also contributed in their own right to our knowledge of the archaeological past. Men and women of the community have excavated numerous archaeological sites in and around town, and, more remarkable still, they pushed for passage of the first national law to protect the country's antiquities.

The pages that follow also tell the story of the dedicated—and sometimes eccentric—characters who put Durango on the archaeological map. In the 1930s, individuals such as Helen Sloan Daniels, Isaiah Ford "Zeke" Flora, and Homer Root learned their archaeology by the seat of their pants. Although they may not always have conducted their excavations or comported themselves as they should have, they paved the way for the professionals who followed in their footsteps.

Another reason for writing this book is that, as archaeologists with some 50 years of combined professional work between us, we believe the public, despite its interest in the past, does not understand exactly what archaeologists currently do; there is still too much of an "Indiana Jones" aura to our profession (an aura, incidentally, that few of us in the field actively discourage). Members of the public also tend to dwell on spectacular ruins and objects, and professionals all too often assume that they won't be interested in the nuts and bolts of the discipline—the thousands of small and unspectacular archaeological sites that truly yield our knowledge of the past (see Box 1.1).

2

BOX 1.1
THE SCOPE OF ARCHAEOLOGY

The term *archaeology* means the study of ancient things, and it is the only science produced by the Western world that can tell us about the human past before writing was invented. Archaeologists concentrate on studying material culture, which is all objects made by humans. These objects, called *artifacts,* include the earliest evidence for humans—bone and worked stone that are millions of years old—and bits of broken pottery made as recently as 50 years ago.

Archaeology is divided into two major subdisciplines. The first subdiscipline, *prehistoric archaeology*, studies people who did not use writing systems, a form of communication that first appeared in the Near East about 6,000 years ago. Because many societies do not need writing to function (its first uses were for such things as religious prophesy and keeping track of taxes), archaeologists are careful not to imply that the use of writing somehow makes one society "better" than another.

The second subdiscipline, *historical archaeology*, uses archaeological techniques as a supplement to historical records and documents. Increasingly, archaeologists are realizing that their discipline can provide insights into literate societies that are often missing in the texts these societies left behind. In the Durango area, for example, only since approximately the mid-1970s have historical archaeologists begun to investigate local mining camps, cabins, and other recent remains. This endeavor has provided information that is missing from the company ledgers and legal documents most commonly used by historians.

All archaeological data are obtained through fieldwork. At first, beginning in the late nineteenth century, archaeologists spent a great deal of time and effort excavating sites that were expected to provide good samples of datable artifacts. In the Southwest, this meant concentrating on large sites that had well-preserved architecture and lots of ceramics.

Only comparatively recently have archaeologists begun to realize that a good deal of information can be acquired simply from surveying the surface of an area and locating the artifacts and sites it contains. Surveys of large regions, sometimes measured by the square mile, give information on the reasons why peoples lived in particular locations and not in others. This information is hard to come by if the archaeologist concentrates on just a few spectacular ruins. The importance of survey data has been accentuated by government-mandated surveys of public land and the rise of the cultural resource management (CRM) industry. Very often, only survey data are available, and archaeologists have developed sophisticated techniques to improve the quality of the inferences that can be drawn from data of this type.

All archaeologists, regardless of their specific interests, have two basic goals. The first is to classify the material that they study and create a sequence for the events of the past. They attempt to develop a *culture history* and try to determine *what* the materials and objects they find are, *who* made them, *when* they were made, and *where* else these objects can be found.

Archaeologists have devised a series of techniques to help them answer the who, what, where, and when questions of their field. The first set of techniques involves classifying the physical traces that past peoples left behind into groups of similar artifacts. Some of these groups are based on obvious criteria—for example, classifying stone tools into projectile points or grinding stones, based on their functions.

Other groupings of artifacts and sites are more complicated. Similar artifacts and sites may have been used in one particular area or region for several hundred years. Such a grouping is called an *archaeological culture*; the Anasazi culture is a very good example of this. Archaeologists, however, still debate why certain similar artifacts and not others were used in a certain area for a certain amount of time. They might ask, for instance, whether a particular pattern was caused by the trading of specific desirable artifacts or if the shared artifacts reflect the remains of a single people or ethnic group.

The second set of techniques involves finding out how old an artifact, site, or culture is. *Relative* dating techniques allow an archaeologist to compare two or more artifacts or sites and determine which is older. Thus, if one excavates an archaeological site, the older artifacts usually are found further from the surface, which allows the archaeologist to determine whether certain artifacts are older or younger than others. *Absolute* dating techniques allow the archaeologist to assign a calendar date to a specific site or artifact—either as B.C., A.D., or B.P. (meaning before the present, which is considered to begin in 1950). Many such techniques are now available, but in the study of Durango archaeology, as in the American Southwest at large, three have been especially useful.

Tree-ring dating, or dendrochronology, is the oldest absolute technique in archaeology. It was developed at the beginning of the twentieth century by an American astronomer, A. E. Douglass. Tree-ring dating relies on the fact that a tree adds another growth ring to its trunk every year. The thickness of this ring is determined by the particular climatic conditions during that year (mainly temperature and rainfall). Because climatic conditions vary from year to year and from place to place, only trees that were growing in the same area and at the same time have identical ring sequences. In the Southwest, where the preservation of wood is excellent, scientists have been able to create master charts of tree-ring sequences, starting in the present day and going back to before the time of Christ.

So, if an archaeologist can recover a piece of well-preserved wood from a site, he or she can compare its tree-ring sequence to the master chart and find out exactly when that tree was growing. If the archaeologist is lucky, the tree will still have enough of its outer layer present to indicate when the tree was actually cut down. Unfortunately, most of the timber used in house beams has had its bark and some of the outer rings removed during the original construction activity, so the outermost ring that is observed may not actually have been the last one formed before the tree was cut down. These *noncutting dates*, therefore, can give the archaeologist only a minimum date for when the tree was cut down. The actual cutting date might have been several years or even decades earlier.

The second technique is radiocarbon dating, developed just after World War II by a University of Chicago physicist, Willard Libby. This technique can be used on any organic material (such as wood and bone), and it can provide reliable dates going back at least 50,000 years. All living things have a certain amount of radioactive carbon in them. At death, this radioactivity begins to decay at a relatively constant rate. Thus, scientists can take a piece of wood or bone, for example, and measure the amount of radioactive carbon left and from that estimate how long ago the plant or animal died. Radiocarbon dating is particularly useful because, unlike tree-ring dating, it can be applied to any organic object anywhere in the world. (For this reason, tree-ring dating is useful only in places such as the Southwest, where prehistoric peoples made extensive use of wood and where the dry climate preserves ancient wood samples.)

The third technique is archeomagnetic dating. This technique is based on the fact that there are iron molecules in most soils. The molecules are attracted to the magnetic North Pole, which moves slightly from year to year. Thus, the angle of orientation of these molecules in the soil also changes each year. If that soil is heated to a high enough temperature, the molecules are no longer magnetically attracted to the North Pole, and they become "locked" into the particular angle at the time of firing. Scientists such as Jeffrey Eighmy of Colorado State University have developed techniques whereby they can analyze the angles of molecules in burned earth, as would be found in and around an ancient hearth. By running archeomagnetic dating and tree-ring dating on the same hearths, archaeologists have been able to determine that, for example, an angle of $11°$ was present in years A.D. 775, 860, and 900. Thus, an archaeologist can date a hearth using this technique and then choose which particular date fits best with other independently derived dating evidence. Archeomagnetic dating is an excellent supplement to other techniques.

The second basic goal for archaeologists is to explain why and how people lived in the past. Since the 1950s, American archaeologists have accomplished this goal by concentrating on ancient peoples' subsistence strategies (i.e., how they got their food) and on how the environment influenced past human behavior. Society is viewed, therefore, as a mechanism by which energy can be extracted from the environment (by hunting or herding animals, by gathering wild plants, or by growing crops) and distributed between its members. In the late 1960s, in a further attempt to explain why cultures did what they did, many archaeologists, especially in North America, launched an effort to make archaeology a "hard" science, relying on rigorous methodologies borrowed from the physical sciences (hypothesis testing, statistical analyses, and so forth). *Processual archaeology*, as it is called, has become an important element of modern archaeology because it allows archaeologists to place much greater confidence in their interpretations.

Recently, some archaeologists have turned their attention to studying the internal makeup of past societies in terms of gender relations and social classes. These *postprocessual* archaeologists are less convinced than the processualists that we can find out the "truth" about the past; indeed, many of them argue that there are numerous interpretations of the past, interpretations that are dependent on the archaeologist's particular political and cultural dispositions. So, for example, the past can be interpreted differently depending on whether the archaeologist is a female or a Native American, a Marxist or a capitalist.

All of us, professional and public alike, must constantly remind ourselves that archaeology can do far more than simply provide stories about how past people lived, fascinating though these stories might be. Today, archaeology is going through an exciting period of change. People in our discipline are questioning just about every assumption our predecessors made, and we are trying to make our work much more relevant to modern society. One of our goals in writing this book is to introduce the public to these new approaches.

We also hope that this volume will indicate the true potential of archaeology. One example of this potential—which will be discussed in greater detail—is suggested by modern archaeologists' reevaluation of the ways in which they work with Native Americans and other indigenous peoples; archaeologists are now more sensitive to the cultures and histories of these individuals. Another example comes from the important lessons archaeology teaches us about utilizing the natural environment. Durango's prehistoric population boom and the resultant crash in the ninth century is a perfect illustration of what can happen when population levels outstrip natural resources. Yet another example of the potential of our field involves the realization that the past is never really over: if how we understand the present is partly dependent on how we understand the past, then the past necessarily intersects the present. So the past lives with us today, and all of us have an influence on how that past is portrayed.

From just about any vantage point in Durango, one can look over the Animas River valley and, despite all the development that has occurred over the past 100 years, get a fair idea of what this beautiful valley looked like centuries ago, long before the Europeans came. Even the newest of newcomers is struck by the sense of timelessness in this lovely little city. There is in Durango a connection to America's past that one rarely finds elsewhere. This book is our personal attempt to convey a sense of this past; to connect the town's European history—and our own—to that of the Pueblo Indians, the Ute and the Navajo, whose ancestors lived in the Animas valley centuries earlier. We hope that those who read the book will begin to see the continuity of history in our towns and neighborhoods and to understand that this continuity joins all of us, regardless of ethnic background, as Americans. Perhaps, too, visitors to our town will come to share our feelings and residents will appreciate their own town's past a little better as well.

One final word is in order here. The book is organized so that different readers can read it in different ways. It is intended primarily for the general reader who may not know much about archaeology but wants to learn more, the reader who is interested in becoming familiar with more than just famous sites of the Southwest. Scattered throughout the book are boxes that give details on specific topics, such as the scope of archaeology or the Basketmaker people. These boxes can be passed over, depending on the reader's level of expertise or interest, without disrupting the book's continuity. Professionals and local amateur archaeologists who want to delve into details such as individual site descriptions can find additional information in the Appendix.

We hope that all readers, regardless of their expertise, will gain a better appreciation of just what lies under present-day Durango and that they will look at their own towns a little differently, too, as they realize that archaeology involves much more than spectacular sites such as Mesa Verde and Chaco Canyon.

2
Southwestern Archaeology

Durango belongs to the geographical-cultural area known as the American Southwest, which stretches from Las Vegas, Nevada, to Las Vegas, New Mexico, and from Durango, Colorado, to Durango, Mexico. Any discussion on the archaeology of Durango must encompass not only the archaeology of the American Southwest but also the archaeology of North America.

Historically, humans on the North American continent made a living in one of two fundamentally different ways. The *hunters and gatherers* (sometimes called *foragers*) fashioned a lifestyle based on hunting various animals and harvesting wild plants. These people were nomadic, living in small family groups and moving with the seasons, and they left behind relatively few material traces of their way of life. The hunter-gatherer tradition was the only way of life on the continent until about 7,000 years ago, and in many areas, it continued until the time of European contact.

The second great tradition was that of the agriculturalists, or the *formative* peoples. Their way of life was based on the planting and harvesting of crops of one kind or another, and it led to the formation of villages and towns. This, in turn, changed the ways in which human societies organized themselves; among agriculturalists in some parts of the world, for example, true economic classes quickly appeared. It also led to the development of long-distance trading networks that enabled the people to access distant resources. People living in farming communities had more time to spend developing specialized crafts such as pottery and basket making, and because farming required them to stay in one place to tend their crops, ancient farmers left behind a much more visible record of their existence, including ceramic vessels, bone and stone tools, and the remains of houses. In the American Southwest and in the Southeast (along the Mississippi River valley), the growing of corn and other crops allowed the development of huge prehistoric towns and cities, which were at their peak just before the Europeans invaded the continent in the sixteenth century.

The culture history of North America is traditionally broken into five periods: *Paleoindian, Archaic, Formative, Late Prehistoric,* and *Historic.* Each of these periods is characterized by different lifestyles and different material cultures, so they are also sometimes called *stages.*

TABLE 2.1 Culture History of the Durango Area

Paleoindian	10,000–5,500 B.C
Archaic	5,500–A.D. 1
Formative: Basketmaker II	A.D. 1–450
Formative: Basketmaker III	A.D. 450–750
Formative: Pueblo I	A.D. 750–900
Formative: Pueblo II	A.D. 900–1150
Formative: Pueblo III	A.D. 1150–1300
Late Prehistoric	A.D. 1200–1765
Historic: European Contact	A.D. 1765–

THE PALEOINDIAN PERIOD (10,000–5,500 B.C.)

The *Ice Age* is the popular term for the geological period called the Pleistocene. The term itself conjure up visions of ice, snow, cold, and Arctic tundra—in sum, a thoroughly hostile and uninviting terrain. The image is unfortunate, however, for this age was, in fact, a time when large animals were available for hunting, and with the right skills and knowledge, individuals must have been able to make a good living. (Interestingly, the Inuit, previously called the Eskimo, do not see the Arctic as forbidding; for them, the land is their home and their provider.)

Archaeologists dispute when the first Americans arrived on the North American continent, with some placing the event as early as 30,000 years ago or more. The traditional view is that humans came to the New World across the Bering Land Bridge, an open piece of tundra millions of square miles in size connecting present-day Alaska and Siberia. The bridge was created by the lowering of sea levels as the huge glaciers that covered the northern half of the Northern Hemisphere sucked up ocean water.

Archaeologists, however, have put forward alternative views. Canadian archaeologist Knut Fladmark, for instance, in a very thoughtful piece written a number of years ago, hypothesized that it was quite feasible that the earliest Native Americans migrated south along the western coastal shelf, an area now under the waters of the eastern Pacific. Unfortunately, finding the archaeological evidence to support this theory is understandably difficult.

The idea that the first Native Americans migrated to the New World, whatever route they took, is entirely archaeological in origin. Many modern Native Americans have a fundamentally different view of their antiquity, believing that their ancestors have *always* lived on this continent. Archaeologists should not lightly dismiss this position, for it is based on deeply held tribal cultural beliefs. Rather, as anthropologists trained to respect other peoples' ways of knowing and interpreting the world, archaeologists should try to understand *why* Native Americans hold this belief; they should also attempt to grasp why it is so important for Native Americans to uphold their own tribal histories as they engage in political and other struggles with Euroamerican society. Discrepancies between archaeological and tribal versions are found throughout the telling of this continent's past. The difficulties in reconciling Native American and Western scientific views on early humans in North America are well illustrated by the Kennewick Man controversy. In 1996, archaeologists discovered a male human skeleton over 9,000 years old in Kennewick, Washington. What made the find controversial is that the skeleton had caucasoid features, a biological category that includes certain south Asian groups and Europeans. Many physical anthropologists wanted total access to the remains to investigate further the hypothesis that the earliest inhabitants of the New World may have been European in origin. This has raised further speculation that the earliest inhabitants of the New World may not have come across the Bering Strait at all; one suggestion is that they may have moved east to west (the Faroe Islands, Greenland, etc.). The local Umatilla Tribe, however, has argued that the skeleton is totally Native American, and, therefore, they have invoked federal law to try to prevent further analysis of the remains and to ensure that the skeleton gets reburied as quickly as possible. They argue that analysis of the skeleton is desecration and must be stopped immediately.

2.1 Paleoindian projectile points. The top one belongs to the Clovis Tradition (11,500–11,000 B.P.), and the bottom is Folsom (11,000–10,000 B.P.).

At the end of the Ice Age, about 12,000 years ago, Paleoindians spread rapidly throughout most of North and South America. These people are identified by the very distinctive projectile points that they made to hunt large animals such as the mammoth, camel, and bison. Hundreds of these beautifully crafted points, used to tip spears and wooden darts, have been found throughout the continent. The most well known of these points are the fluted Clovis and Folsom points (Figure 2.1), named after the localities in New Mexico where they were first found. (*Flute* is the name given to the long flake that was removed from each point's body, probably in the process of hafting the point to the shaft.) These points were flaked by their knappers with a precision that went well beyond what was needed to make the points functional. Archaeologists speculate, therefore, that the points had a symbolic importance, as well, perhaps related to death and killing. Paleoindian sites, whether the remains of campsites where small bands of people lived or kill sites where animals were actually slain and butchered, are rare finds. Also, because of the paucity of evidence, it is difficult to estimate the relative importance of gathered plants in the total diet of the Paleoindians.

There are three subperiods within the larger Paleoindian period: Clovis, Folsom, and Plano. Clovis people were primarily mammoth hunters. By the following Folsom period, however, large bison were the most important prey, as the end of the Ice Age had extinguished the other large animals that once flourished in the colder temperatures of that time. Finds from the Plano period exhibit the greatest diversity in terms of the types of projectile points made, perhaps because the larger populations in that period led to a fragmentation of human groups into distinctive territories with distinctive technologies.

Although the Archaic period replaced the Paleoindian period in many parts of the continent, in some places, most notably the Plains, big-game hunting continued until the Euroamerican invasion of the eighteenth century.

THE ARCHAIC PERIOD (5,500 B.C.–A.D. 1)

In general parlance, *archaic* is a pejorative word, so it is unfortunate that it is applied to a group of people who practiced a sustained and, therefore, well-adapted lifestyle. Nonetheless, the term has been used by archaeologists for so many years that it is difficult to avoid using it in a work of this type.

In southwestern Colorado, the Archaic period extended from about 7,500 years ago to around the time of Christ, but in many parts of the United States, most notably in Utah and Nevada, an Archaic lifestyle was practiced until the Historic period.

The Archaic period is the least-known archeological era among the public. In part, this is because Archaic life was unspectacular, judging by what remains in the archaeological record. Tool kits from this period were usually fairly functional, typically consisting of one-handed *manos* (grinding stones) for grinding seeds and other products, flat sheets of rock called *metates* used in conjunction with the manos, chipped projectile points, knives and scraping tools, and vast amounts of waste flakes left over from the preparation of stone tools (these flakes are called *debitage*). However, in a few dry caves, archaeologists have found spectacular examples of well-preserved baskets, sandals, sashes, nets, and other carefully crafted tools made from plant fiber and leaf. Unfortunately, however, such objects of everyday Archaic life generally did not survive the harsher environments of southwestern Colorado.

When the specialized and highly distinctive Paleoindian projectile points were no longer being manufactured, a differently shaped point, with either a side notch or a corner notch, appeared throughout Colorado and most of the West. Many of these Archaic points are very distinctive and help identify both the time period and the geographic location in which they were made. For example, points from

2.2 Rare Pueblo III bowl. Note the corrugated exterior and painted interior. Courtesy, Center of Southwest Studies, Fort Lewis College.

the Plains are clearly distinct from contemporary points in the Great Basin.

These points were used not as spear tips but as part of the *atlatl* technology. In this system, a hunter used a throwing stick as a means of launching a projectile through the air. The throwing stick was a long piece of wood, into which the projectile was fitted. The stick was then used essentially as an extension of the hunter's arm to increase the projectile's velocity and accuracy.

Although animals killed by hunting still made a significant contribution to the Archaic diet, archaeologists think that the people of this period practiced a generalized hunting-and-gathering strategy in which a wide range of animals—from large deer and elk to small rabbits—were stalked and many wild plants were collected. A heavier use of plant foods is reflected in the increase in stone grinding tools during the Archaic period.

THE FORMATIVE PERIOD (A.D. 1–1300)

The Archaic period was followed by the Formative period. The lifestyle of this period began in Mexico, where corn was first

BOX 2.1
THE ANASAZI or ANCESTRAL PUEBLO

The Anasazi was a Formative-level prehistoric tradition found in a particular geographic area (the Four Corners region) during a particular time period (about 2,000 years ago); it incorporated a particular set of artifacts and architectural styles that, despite some variation, show a great deal of continuity through the centuries. The word *Anasazi* comes from a Navajo word that has been variously translated as "Ancient Ones" and "Enemy Ancestors". As we shall see later, many Native Americans in the Four Corners area wish to drop this term, in place of a more culturally sensitive one, although a replacement has not been decided upon by all parties.

The Anasazi tradition is thought to represent the archaeological remains of the modern-day Pueblo Indians, such as the Hopi, Zuni, and Jemez tribes, who now live in New Mexico and Arizona. However, the Navajo also make claims on some Anasazi sites, and so the matter is not yet settled.

The tradition is divided by archaeologists into a number of smaller periods: Basketmaker II and III and Pueblo I, II, III, and IV. These periods show an increasing reliance on agriculture, larger settlement sizes, and the development of more and more complex technology and crafts. Some of the most spectacular sites and artifacts of the tradition belong to the Pueblo III period (A.D. 1150–1300). The discovery of Cliff Palace at Mesa Verde National Park (Figure 2.3) was one of the turning points in the study and preservation of the Southwest's antiquities, and impressive pottery, like the one shown in Figure 2.2, stimulated worldwide interest in the region.

Most of the archaeological sites in Durango and the Animas valley belong to the Basketmaker II and III and early Pueblo I periods. At the start of the ninth century, the Durango area was abandoned by the Anasazi. About A.D. 1300, the rest of the Four Corners region was abandoned, perhaps, according to Hopi histories, with people moving off in small clan groups. In time, the Anasazi reformed into the villages that were found by the Spanish in the late 1500s and early 1600s and that are still inhabited by their descendants, the Pueblo Indians.

2.3 Cliff Palace, Mesa Verde National Park. Courtesy, Mesa Verde National Park.

domesticated about 7,000 years ago, and in the last few centuries before Christ, the way of life spread rapidly. Formative peoples constructed permanent homes and developed crafts such as basket and pottery making. In addition, the atlatl was replaced by the true bow and arrow (see Box 2.1 and Figures 2.2 and 2.3).

THE LATE PREHISTORIC PERIOD (A.D. 1–1765)

Although agriculture became the most important way of getting food in many parts of the continent, Native Americans did not adopt the new agriculturalist lifestyle unless it made sense to them. Consequently, in places such as the Great Plains, prehistoric Indians continued their hunting-and-gathering lifestyle, although they did adopt the bow and arrow and, in some cases, make pottery. Archaeologists assign such non-Formative-level peoples of the last 2,000 years of prehistory to the Late Prehistoric period.

Groups like the Ute moved into southwestern Colorado at least 1,000 years ago, and their archaeological remains are assigned to the Late Prehistoric period. However, they may have been here much longer; certainly, the Ute themselves believe so. Members of this tribe were the primary occupants of southwest Colorado until they were forced onto reservations in the nineteenth century.

THE HISTORIC PERIOD (A.D. 1765–)

The Historic period is marked by the arrival of the Europeans on the North American continent. Ultimately, the European incursion led to the removal of aboriginal inhabitants to reservations and to attempts to destroy their cultures. No amount of whitewashing—whether by 1930s Hollywood movies or recent revisionist histories—alters this simple fact: European-Americans took land that wasn't theirs, and when they couldn't pursue genocidal policies, they pushed the original inhabitants onto reservations.

Archaeologists recognize the Historic period by the appearance of European-manufactured goods, such as the gun and other metal objects, and the reintroduction of the horse, which had become extinct in North America at the end of the Ice Age. Equally as important, Europeans introduced writing to the continent, which meant that modern scholars would have an additional source of information about life in this period—documents that describe the aboriginal peoples.

The introduction of manufactured goods and writing were important changes, to be sure, but they must be viewed in perspective. We must understand that Native American cultures do not consider the arrival of Europeans as a great leap forward, and, as Native American elders have explained to us, they feel no need to divide the past into prehistoric and historic components. Native American cultures still flourish; they are not relics of the past.

Historical archaeology, the term applied to the archaeological investigation of Historic-period peoples, is not limited to the study of the historical past of Native American groups. On the contrary, a major emphasis in this field is on the early histories of European communities in North America. Historical archaeology thus can often give a dimension to past life that isn't revealed in the dry ledgers and dockets of mining companies and ranches. There is more than a little truth in the old archaeological adage that history tends to study the rich and famous whereas historical archaeology looks at everybody else.

3.1 View from south of town looking north up the Animas valley.

3
Durango's Past

Beneath the houses, offices, and roads of modern Durango are a host of archaeological sites; in fact, the town is literally built on the archaeological remains of past inhabitants. In this chapter, we will offer an overview of these remains, referring interested readers to the detailed descriptions of the individual sites included in the Appendix.

The lifestyle of the early residents of Durango was heavily influenced by the natural environment, as is the case today, and the Animas River was of utmost importance. In addition to attracting animals such as elk and deer and providing humans with water, the river and its valley also served as a corridor between the dry deserts to the south and the wetter mountains to the north, again just as it does today. Consequently, prehistoric inhabitants who lived in the Durango area had relatively easy access to both environments and their different resources, and, as we shall discuss, these upper reaches of the Animas valley often served as a refuge for people escaping the harsher climatic conditions that sometimes existed in areas to the south.

The dominance of the river over the valley and its importance as a communication corridor between the deserts and the mountains is illustrated in Figure 3.1. Figure 3.2 shows the terraces that flanked both sides of the river and provided homes for ancient peoples, much as they do today.

Much of the following information on the glacial chronology was originally compiled by Jeri Smalley as part of a synthesis of archaeological resources on the San Juan National Forest. Between 40,000 to

3.2 View southeast over the Riverview and Crestview subdivisions.

11,000 years ago, most of the high mountain valleys of Colorado contained glaciers. Of all of the ranges in the state, the San Juans had the most extensive glaciers, probably because of the heavier overall precipitation in the area. (This is characteristic of the San Juans even today. The Wolf Creek Ski Area, 70 miles east of Durango, has the deepest snow of any ski area in the United States; a base of 100 inches of snow is normal.)

At least six glacial periods affected the San Juan Mountains during the last 2 million years, although there actually may have been fifteen or more. The Animas glacier was one of the longest in the southern Rockies, stretching from Silverton to Durango, a distance of over 40 miles. Today, the Equilibrium Line Altitude (ELA), the line above which snow and ice accumulate faster than they melt and which corresponds roughly to the permanent snow line, lies at an elevation of about 12,200 feet. About 18,000 B.P. (meaning "before the present"), however, the ELA was as much as 2,000 feet lower. Thus, above about 10,000 feet, permanent snow and ice entirely shut off the higher San Juans area to human exploitation.

3.3 Animas City (present-day north Durango) in 1897. The terminal moraine is clearly visible in this photograph. Notice also the sparseness of the vegetation and the course of the river, well to the east of its present course. Photograph by Whitman Cross. Courtesy, La Plata County Historical Society.

The effects of the glaciers are still evident. Glaciers are like massive, slow-moving bulldozers that push soil and rock ahead of them, fundamentally altering the ground surface for thousands of years. After the glaciers retreated, they left behind a terminal moraine (a ridge of boulders and sediments lying across the valley). In Durango, the low east-west ridge that runs along 32nd Street is such a geological feature (Figure 3.3).

In general, the glaciers had the effect of moving vegetation communities down in elevation. For example, about 15,000 B.P., the climate of the Durango area, at an elevation of 6,500' above sea level (asl), approximated that of Molas Pass today, which lies at an elevation of 10,910' asl. At that time, musk oxen grazed on the flats at the foot of the glacier.

During the last stages of the Pleistocene, the Animas valley and the surrounding land would have looked quite different from the way it does today. The valley probably contained a melting glacier and a much larger river that meandered from one side of the valley to the other. The spruce-fir forest found today at higher elevations in the San Juan Mountains would have covered the slopes of the hillsides above the valley and probably continued down the valley for many miles to the south. There would have been many swamps and lakes. On and around these wetlands would be flocks of birds and waterfowl. Snow and ice would have lasted much longer during the year; indeed, snowfields on the hillsides above the valley in May and even June would not have been unusual.

As the climate became warmer, the glacier began to retreat back up the valley, and over time, it melted entirely until, about 8,000 years ago, the valley began to look much as it does today. Interestingly, the valley bottom was probably never as heavily covered by trees as it is now, as shown by a late-nineteenth-century photograph of early Durango taken from the north end of town. The abundant trees that town residents enjoy today are mostly the result of European settlement and the desire to re-create an eastern environment.

As it winds through the Durango area, the Animas River valley is still flanked by flat terraces that were formed during the last Ice Age. These terraces are now covered by the various subdivisions—primarily Crestview on the west and Riverview on the east—that were developed after World War II to house Durango's growing population. These same terraces also housed substantial prehistoric populations, especially during the seventh and eighth centuries.

Even though the end of the Ice Age generally brought a modern climate and environment to the area, there were still local fluctuations. A number of years ago, Colorado archaeologist John Gooding, using data provided by Jeffrey Dean and other scientists at the Arizona State Museum, showed that Durango has regularly experienced hotter-drier and colder-wetter climatic cycles, averaging several hundred years in length. This occasionally caused more than a slight problem for the ancient farmers who eventually settled in the valley.

SITES FROM THE PALEOINDIAN PERIOD

The classic Paleoindian sites of North America are located on the western plains of the continent. However, in the mountain-foothills areas of Colorado and Wyoming, Paleoindian points are being found in increasing numbers. The projectile points from these areas (which include Durango) have several distinct characteristics. They are generally more roughly made than those from other locales, and they are often crafted out of materials such as quartzite, which does not produce the thin, finely chipped points typically found on the Plains. The people who made them were probably generalized hunters and gatherers, rather than big-game hunters.

Recent studies of Paleoindian remains in the San Juan National Forest have shown that although there was a harsh climate in the region, the area was probably inhabited by Paleoindian hunters and gatherers. None of the finds are Clovis or Folsom; rather, all but one belong to the Plano tradition. The exception is the famous Black Mountain site located 65 miles northeast of Durango close to the town of Creede at an altitude of 10,160 feet asl, near the headwaters of the Rio Grande. That site, found in 1977, has been excavated since 1993 by a team from the Smithsonian Institution, under the direction of Margaret Jodry and Dennis Stanford. Thus far, it has yielded portions of 5 Folsom preforms (i.e., unfinished points), numerous stone tools, and over 1,000 flakes. Black Mountain, the highest-altitude Folsom site yet found, clearly shows that Paleoindian peoples were utilizing the high country.

To date, very few traces of the Paleoindian period have been discovered in the Durango area. There are many reasons for this. For one thing, the environment mitigates against such finds. Even today in southwest Colorado, the mountains are still being actively eroded, which means that most Paleoindian sites would have been destroyed, partially or totally, by ongoing erosion. Then, too, when soil deposition does occur in the area, it is usually a very slow process and the deposits are typically very thin, which also contributed to the fragility of ancient sites.

In addition, Paleoindian sites are usually small and hard to find, and so they are easily overlooked by most people except the professional. In fact, discoveries of these sites are more often the result of luck rather than any deliberate strategy employed by archaeologists.

Paleoindian sites may also have been collected by later Indian peoples. In the mountains surrounding Durango, U.S. Forest Service (USFS) archaeologists have found isolated Paleoindian points on much more recent sites, suggesting that later Native Americans picked up the early points (just as we do today) and either reused them or kept them as curiosities.

Finally, most of the archaeological sites in Durango were found by amateurs who were interested primarily in large Anasazi ruins, with their well-made pithouses and pottery. It would have been easy for them to overlook a small Paleoindian site lying next to a more impressive Anasazi pithouse.

Recently, two archaeologists have examined the information researchers have accumulated about the Paleoindian period in this part of the world. Initially, Bob York, who served as the archaeologist for the San Juan National Forest for many years, studied all of the points that have been found in that forest. Bonnie Pitblado then expanded upon that study in her master's thesis at the University of Arizona, including all of the points found in southwestern Colorado. These two works give us a fairly good idea of the nature of the Paleoindians' use of and occupation in the Durango area. Two important conclusions have resulted.

First, we have learned that Paleoindian peoples were rarely, if at all, present in the San Juan Mountains and the Animas valley before about 10,000 years ago. Specifically, the Clovis and Folsom peoples who were so prominent on the Plains were rare visitors to the mountains of southwest Colorado. Thus, it appears that the primary use of the Durango and mountain areas of southwest Colorado probably did not occur until the Plano period, which began about 10,000 years ago. The second broad conclusion is that the Paleoindian peoples who did make regular intrusions into southwestern Colorado and the mountains had a separate cultural tradition from those living in the Plains and the Great Basin.

Despite the minimal use made of the Durango area by Paleoindian peoples, remains from these individuals are not entirely absent. A small number of Paleoindian points have been found very close to Durango. The oldest is a complete Clovis point that, according to our informant, was found on a mesa just south of town. Unfortunately, the exact location of the site was never divulged to us, and so our knowledge of the point is minimal. However, if the information is accurate, that artifact is the only Clovis point documented from southwestern Colorado. This may mean that Clovis people passed briefly through the Durango area or that later peoples picked up the point and dropped it at that location. (Incidentally, this is an excellent example of why the seemingly innocent practice of collecting so-called arrowheads or projectile points can be highly detrimental to our knowledge of the past. Such artifacts could be critical links to the beginnings of human history in a specific area.)

A second projectile point was recently turned over to Fort Lewis College by a local resident. This point was apparently first found about 50 years ago in the Breen area, southwest of Durango, and had been gathering dust on a mantelpiece ever since. The point has been identified by Bruce Bradley of Cortez, one of the country's leading Paleoindian experts, as the base of a Folsom point. It was made of Dakota sandstone and so may have been crafted locally.

A third article, a Plano point (Plainview type), was found in the Falls Creek valley by Fort Lewis College archaeologist W. James "Jim" Judge in 1991. Interestingly enough, this makes Falls Creek not only the oldest Anasazi site in southwestern Colorado but also one of the oldest known locations of Paleoindian peoples in this region.

Isolated Paleoindian points have also been found in Ridges Basin, a few miles south of Durango. However, these were interpreted as having been reused by later peoples, according to John Ware, a New Mexico archaeologist who conducted important studies in Ridges Basin in the early 1980s. One of these points has been identified by Francis Smiley, the lead investigator in ongoing, federally sponsored archaeological work in the basin, as possibly a Hell Gap type.

Sites From the Archaic Period

U.S. Forest Service archaeologists have discovered hundreds of Archaic sites in the mountains to the north of Durango, but there are very few at lower elevations. At Mesa Verde National Park, for example, where some 5,000 archaeological sites have been recorded, there is only one site that park archaeologists are willing to assign to the Archaic period. The few Archaic sites known in the Durango area are mostly limited to the west end of Ridges Basin. In Bodo Canyon, just south of town, archaeologist Steve Fuller excavated three Late Archaic site components that dated to between 1 and 500 B.C. Two of the sites were short-term hunting camps, and one was possibly used as a camp for gathering plants.

Based on this evidence, then, it is probable that Archaic peoples

PITHOUSE: 5LP119 (BODO AREA)

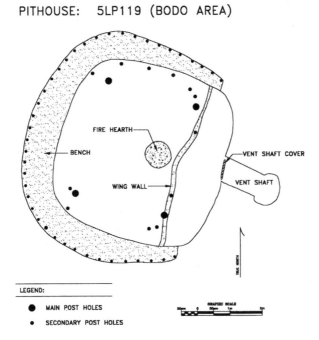

LEGEND:

● MAIN POST HOLES

• SECONDARY POST HOLES

3.4 Plan of pithouse 5LP 119, located in the Bodo area at the south end of town. Courtesy, Department of Anthropology, Fort Lewis College.

passed through the Animas valley during their seasonal nomadic movements. However, archaeologists do not have a particularly good understanding of the specifics of the Archaic occupation of the Durango area, and there are still many more questions than answers. Are Archaic sites deeply buried in places where archaeologists have not yet looked? Did Archaic peoples even live at the same lower elevations as the Anasazi? Did the Anasazi collect the Archaic remains? Did the Anasazi build their sites on top of the Archaic sites, causing the Archaic materials to be "absorbed" into the much more numerous artifacts left behind by Anasazi occupants? And how many Archaic sites have been destroyed by later European construction?

SITES FROM THE FORMATIVE PERIOD

The vast majority of known archaeological sites in Durango are Anasazi, and most of these belong to the Basketmaker III and early

BOX 3.1
THE BASKETMAKER III PEOPLE

The term *Basketmaker* is a bit of a misnomer in describing these people because Basketmaker III sites are actually characterized by pottery, rather than baskets. The standard Basketmaker dwelling is called a pithouse (Figure 3.4). As the name implies, the structure is a circular or rectangular pit excavated up to 2 meters below the ground surface. The floor and walls were often plastered with mud, and sometimes a bench of earth (sometimes called a *banquette*) was built around the inner wall. This served not only as a storage shelf but also as a support for posts that held up the wooden roof. The pithouse had a central fireplace, and sometimes a ventilator shaft was dug through the wall of the pithouse to the surface, providing a flow of fresh air. To keep this draft from scattering the fire and smoke everywhere, an upright deflector slab of sandstone was set in place. In some cases, internal adobe wall partitions were built in the pithouse (these are called wing walls). Storage pits and perhaps even a *sipapu* (symbolizing the Pueblo peoples' sacred point of emergence into the present world) were sometimes excavated into the floor. The pithouse was very thermally efficient, but because of its wooden construction, it was prone to burning down. The pithouse was surrounded by storage pits or, in later periods (and this is well exemplified in Durango), by surface rooms made of branches and beams covered in *jacal* ("adobe").

The Basketmakers made gray-colored pottery, which was sometime decorated with black paint in various motifs (Figures 3.5, 3.6, and 3.7). They grew corn, although they almost certainly relied heavily on hunting and gathering, too. They also used the bow and arrow, as opposed to the earlier atlatl; this is indicated by the smaller projectile points found in Basketmaker III sites.

Pueblo I periods. Between about A.D. 650 and 800, it has been estimated, literally hundreds of Basketmaker III and Pueblo I pithouses were built. Many of these sites are now under the modern town of Durango, but since the 1930s, many have been recorded by archaeologists and quite a few have been excavated (see Box 3.1 and Figures 3.4 through 3.7).

3.5 Basketmaker III grayware pottery. The double bowl is of unknown provenience, and the two others were recovered from 5LP 119. Courtesy, Center of Southwest Studies and the Department of Anthropology, Fort Lewis College.

John Ware has suggested that the majority of pithouses in the Durango area are transitional Basketmaker III–Pueblo I types. Several features of the pithouses contribute to this assessment: they lack the southern recesses characteristic of Basketmaker III pithouses in the La Plata and Mesa Verde districts; most of them have true tunnel ventilator shafts, which are characteristic of Pueblo I construction; and they appear to cluster into communities, again similar to Pueblo I patterns. That many of them date to the second half of the eighth century also suggests the transitional nature of these sites.

Although pithouses are found throughout the Animas valley and Durango, there seem to be distinct concentrations of Anasazi sites throughout this region—such as in Falls Creek, Ridges Basin, Blue Mesa, Bodo Industrial Park, College Mesa, and Crestview (Figures 3.8 and 3.9). It is unclear, however, whether these concentrations represent the actual distribution of the prehistoric population or whether they are simply reflections of the areas that archaeologists have thus far had a chance to study.

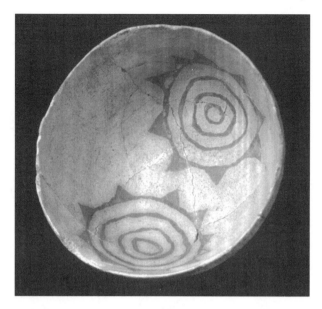

3.6 Basketmaker III black-on-gray bowl. Note that during this period, the decoration consisted of individual motifs, rather than the later style of treating the whole vessel as a single compositional unit. Courtesy, Center of Southwest Studies, Fort Lewis College.

3.7 Basketmaker III black-on-gray bowl. This remarkable bowl is decorated with anthropomorphic figures. It is interesting to speculate that the central figure has hair whorls similar to those depicted in Historic period photographs of Hopi girls. Courtesy, Center of Southwest Studies, Fort Lewis College.

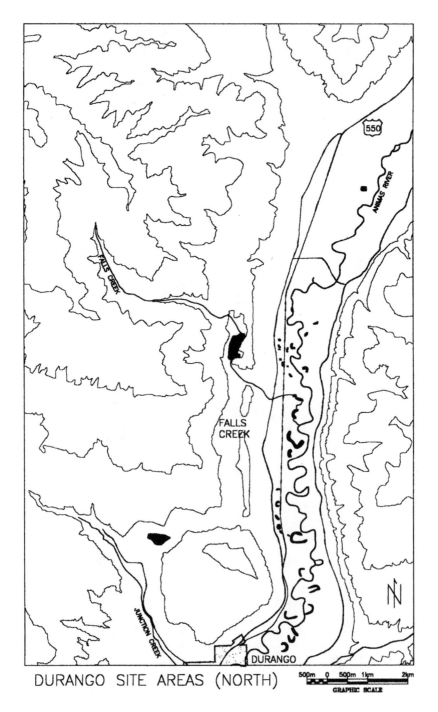

DURANGO SITE AREAS (NORTH)

500m 0 500m 1km 2km
GRAPHIC SCALE

3.8 Map of north Durango.

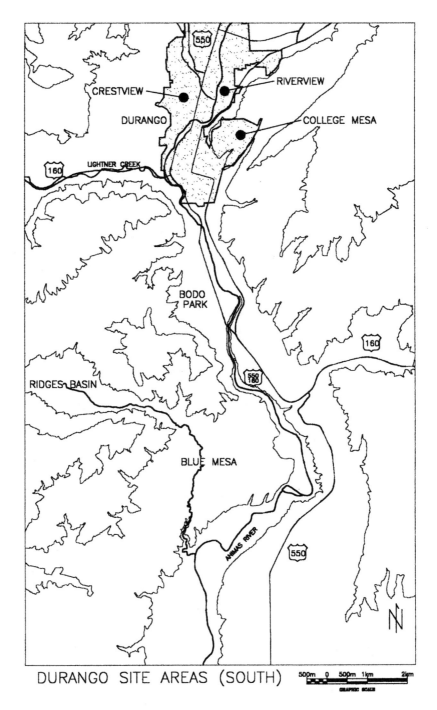

DURANGO SITE AREAS (SOUTH)

3.9 Map of south Durango.

FALLS CREEK AND TALUS VILLAGE

By far the most important archaeological discovery in Durango is that of the Falls Creek Rock Shelters. Falls Creek is a small valley to the north and west of Durango and the Animas valley. With a broad, flat floor that is perfect for farming, the Falls Creek valley is not visible from the main Animas valley, and so it was named Hidden Valley by local residents sometime around the turn of the twentieth century. The shelters there were once known to locals as Esther's Cave, but information on the excavations that were ultimately conducted at the site was published under the title of *The Durango Rock Shelters* by Earl Morris and his assistant Robert Burgh. In 1993, the U.S. Forest Service, on whose land the shelters lay, created the Falls Creek Archaeological Area to preserve the shelters and to provide for public access. As a result, Falls Creek is the name that is likely to endure.

The archaeological site itself consists of two rock shelters at the base of a thick, sheer cliff made of Entrada sandstone. These are called the North Shelter and the South Shelter, and both are visible from the bottom of Falls Creek. Based on the tree-ring dates obtained from the sites, the heaviest occupation of the sites occurred about A.D. 50; the total occupation range for the area spanned approximately from 300 B.C. to A.D. 300.

Helen Sloan Daniels apparently told Zeke Flora, another local amateur archaeologist, about the two rock shelters, as well as some nearby prehistoric rock art. Flora visited the shelters and immediately began excavating in areas that he thought would produce artifacts or wood specimens. He probed a narrow crack in the back of the North Shelter and found a natural burial "vault." Before the day was over, he had found two human bodies, desiccated and discolored but as perfectly preserved as any human mummy found anywhere in the world to date. One was that of a young woman; the other was a boy in his teens. The woman had short black hair and wore a woven pubic sash. She had been placed in the crack with both legs drawn up behind her, and her hands were tied and crossed in front of her. The body was wrapped in a rabbit-skin robe and lay on a bed of soft juniper bark. Less is known about the circumstances of the adolescent boy. Flora also found a variety of rare artifacts, including jewelry, sandals, baskets, and other items.

At the end of the day, Flora hauled the two ancient bodies through the thick oak brush and down the slope to the valley below, losing some of the associated artifact material and damaging the bodies in the process. Once home, he began to realize what he had discovered. It dawned on him that in his initial excavations, he had found no pottery; therefore, the site had to predate nearly all of the known Anasazi remains yet found in southwestern Colorado. Only in the deep and remote Tsegi Canyon system of northeastern Arizona had similar remains and artifacts been discovered.

Within a week, Flora had shared news of his find with Earl Morris from the Carnegie Institution and the University of Colorado. Morris, recognizing the possible importance of the discovery, arrived in Durango in September 1937 to view the finds. Unfortunately, he was unable to examine them directly because the Flora home was under medical quarantine at the time, but Morris saw enough to convince him that further excavations were warranted.

Morris's interest lay in the fact that the caves almost certainly contained Basketmaker II or earlier materials. This was especially exciting because, at that time, although sufficient information had been gathered to confirm most of the period of Anasazi history, the Basketmaker II period was only known from a few caves in Arizona that Alfred V. Kidder and his associates had excavated in the early part of the twentieth century. Moreover, there was also a search on for the hypothetical Basketmaker I period. We now know that the period does not exist in the form anticipated, but Morris did not know this, and to him, it seemed entirely possible that the Falls Creek Rock Shelters would provide that long-sought information on the Basketmaker I period. In addition, Morris was interested in the types of house structures that might have been used during this period, and the site also promised to provide critical wood specimens to help lengthen the tree-ring chronology being developed for the American Southwest.

Morris, along with his assistant, Robert Burgh, and Zeke Flora, began excavations at the North Shelter in 1938. He knew that time was of the essence because as word of the find spread, the area would become increasingly vulnerable to looting. During the next two seasons, Morris conducted extensive excavations in the North Shelter, the South Shelter, and eventually at a small site at the base of the cliffs along the Animas River called Talus Village (its original site number is Ignacio

7:101). A more detailed description of the site, the recovered remains of forty-four humans, and their artifacts can be found in the Appendix.

The remains of the young woman and the boy found by Flora were eventually transferred to Mesa Verde National Park, over Zeke's vehement protests. There, they were exhibited as "Esther" and "Jasper" (unfortunate Anglo names having nothing whatsoever to do with their true ethnic affiliation, of course) until an offended and outraged Native American community asked that they be removed from the view of gawking tourists visiting the park. Today, they are housed at the research center at Mesa Verde, pending a decision on their final resting place. Under the provisions of the Native American Graves Protection and Repatriation Act (NAGPRA), the closest descendants of the young woman and the boy will determine where they should be reburied. Perhaps, one day they will be returned to the Falls Creek Rock Shelters, thus ending an intellectual and moral journey that began 50 years ago.

Unfortunately, a combination of time and the destructive effects of the initial excavations has left very little of the Falls Creek site for the visitor to see. A few of the house floors still exist, but these were recently covered by the U.S. Forest Service to prevent them from being damaged by vandals, foot traffic, and natural processes.

Today, the site is on the National Register of Historic Places and, as noted, is preserved by the U.S. Forest Service as the Falls Creek Archaeological Area. In 1994 and 1995, the Friends of the Durango Rock Shelters tracked down most of the skeletal material and artifacts from the area, as well as an extensive body of correspondence written during the excavations. This work was done by John Sanders, Ernie Cotton, Reid Ross, and Gary Matlock, with a grant from the Colorado Historical Society.

The excavations at Falls Creek produced a great deal of new information on the Basketmaker peoples in Durango, but Earl Morris was left frustrated by one aspect of the work. Although he had found the first substantial floors from these earliest of structures in the Southwest, he was unable to determine what the superstructure that covered the floors looked like. He was determined to find a site that would have evidence for the walls and roofs of these buildings.

So, in 1939, Morris began a search for additional Basketmaker sites that might provide more information on the house types. With the assistance of Flora, he excavated a series of Basketmaker III sites at the north end of Hidden Valley. A total of six sites were excavated, and others were recorded. Many of these sites are now located within the Falls Creek Community housing development. Although Morris was not able to find additional information about Basketmaker II house types, he did find new information on the Basketmaker III period.

Unfortunately, on his return to the University of Colorado (CU) in Boulder, his interest in the Falls Creek Rock Shelters and the importance of preparing a publication on them led him to neglect the analysis of the Basketmaker III sites. In 1961, a few years after Morris's death, CU hired Roy Carlson, a young archaeologist from Arizona, to complete the work on Falls Creek. His synthesis of Morris's notes was published two years later. Carlson recently retired as professor of archaeology at Simon Fraser University in British Columbia, after a distinguished career in the discipline.

In 1940, on the recommendation of Daniels and Flora, Morris turned his attention to Talus Village, a site located outside of Hidden Valley within the Animas valley itself and not far from the present location of the Trimble Hot Springs. He was still seeking the elusive Basketmaker II house structure. The excavations here proved successful in that Morris was able to find evidence that the Basketmaker II structures had been covered by a cribbed timber roof. Confirmation of this form of wall construction was found years later by archaeologist Alan Reed at the Tamarron site, about 10 miles to the north. Wood fragments and poles helped establish the tree-ring calendar for the early part of the first millennium, and these specimens remain some of the most important acquired by the Tree Ring Laboratory at the University of Arizona.

In the early 1960s, Robert Lister excavated a Basketmaker II site in Falls Creek (Ignacio 12:46). The site comprised an oval living floor of beaten earth associated with eight cists and a central depression. Wood beams were probably part of a cribbed roof structure. It was likely built in the middle of the fourth century, and as such, it is the most recent Basketmaker II house discovered in the Durango area. The Darkmold site, located on private property just north of Durango, promises much new information on Basketmaker II occupation. As of 1998, a number of features, including a large pithouse, had been recovered, along with numerous human burials.

Sporadic reports of additional early Basketmaker II and Basketmaker III sites continue to be made in Durango, but the extent of the Basketmaker II occupation and the use made of the upper Animas valley by the early residents are still not fully clear. In 1994, the U.S. Forest Service began a complete survey of the portions of Falls Creek included within the Falls Creek Archaeological Area, and USFS staff members have recorded additional sites, all of which are from the Basketmaker II and Basketmaker III periods.

Falls Creek was abandoned by the Anasazi people by about A.D. 800, and apparently, the Anasazi never returned to live in the valley. A single stone structure on the ridge between the Falls Creek valley and the Animas River valley to the east may be from a later date and may indicate that the Anasazi visited or even lived in the valley for a short time during the late Pueblo I or Pueblo II period. However, no excavations or studies have been conducted on this small site, and its date and use are yet to be determined.

RIDGES BASIN

In the late 1970s, Ridges Basin was surveyed by a team of professional archaeologists to assess the impact that the construction of a proposed reservoir (associated with a federally funded water conservation project called the Animas–La Plata Project) would have on archaeological sites in the basin. Kent Leidy, a consulting archaeologist, was contracted to survey portions of the basin in 1975, and he located 37 sites, of which 4 were Anglo sites from the Historic period. A subsequent comprehensive survey of Ridges Basin and the adjacent sections of Upper Wildcat Canyon by the ESCA-TECH Corporation located 193 archaeological sites, ranging from Paleoindian to Historic Euroamerican: 36 Euroamerican, 15 possible Ute, 12 Late Pueblo I–Pueblo III, 105 Transitional Basketmaker-Pueblo, and 25 possible Basketmaker II, Archaic, or Paleoindian. A magnetometer survey of selected sites was also completed, enabling researchers to read anomalies in the earth's magnetic field caused by underground structures such as pithouses; this technique allows archaeologists to see what is the under the surface without actually digging.

Although the ESCA-TECH survey was the first comprehensive review of the area, the basin had long been a focus of interest for amateur archaeologists such as Homer Root. Indeed, it was Root's work

in Ridges Basin that helped usher in the modern era of Durango archaeology. Root was a retired Methodist minister who organized Fort
Lewis College's first archaeological field schools in Ridges Basin. He
had been active in Durango archaeology since the 1930s, and his goal
in Ridges Basin reflected these beginnings: to excavate large pithouses
that were architecturally complex and that had the potential for yielding good museum-quality pottery.

In 1965, 1966, 1967, and 1969, Root and a crew of students excavated a series of spectacular Basketmaker III pithouses that dated to
the seventh and eighth centuries. In all, 5 deep pit structures, 2 shallow, circular structures, 51 surface structures, and numerous trash
middens (essentially, shallow garbage dumps) were excavated. Root
was assiduous in recording his research in lavishly illustrated portfolios. These portfolios, together with his unedited field notes, photographs, and even a series of 8-mm videos of his excavations are currently housed in the Center of Southwest Studies at Fort Lewis College.

Partly as a result of the interest in Root's work, Fort Lewis College
decided to expand its archaeology offerings. In 1966, the school hired
John Ives, a graduate of Harvard University, as its first professionally
trained archaeologist. Ives worked in Ridges Basin with the college's
field school in 1967 and 1968 and excavated a series of pithouse com-
plexes that were contemporary with Root's sites.

In 1981, the Fort Lewis College field school, under the direction
of Philip Duke and Jamie Karlson, returned to Ridges Basin. The school
excavated sites 5LP 630 and 5LP 242, a pithouse complex dating to
the end of the eighth century. The college's field school excavations
in 1982, directed by Philip Duke and Susan M. Riches, were an extension of the previous year's work and were aimed at investigating sites
located in the pinon-juniper zone at a slightly higher elevation than
the others that had been excavated.

Later in the 1980s, Ridges Basin and the adjacent Bodo Canyon
were visited again by archaeologists as a result of the proposed removal
of the vast pile of mine tailings left at the old Durango Smelter at the
south end of town. The smelter had been used to recover first vana-
dium and then uranium in the 1940s and 1950s. The pile was radioactive, and the federal government proposed to move all the tailings
into Bodo Canyon as a part of a national program to clean up toxic-
waste dumps.

Bodo Canyon was resurveyed by archaeologists from the consulting firm of Nickens and Associates (the fieldwork was directed by
Gary Matlock, and the subsequent report was prepared by Susan Chandler). A total of 24 new sites were found and recorded, 5 already known
sites were rerecorded (these had first been located by Flora and Root),
and 12 isolated finds were discovered. In 1985 and 1986, Steven Fuller,
working with the firm of Complete Archaeological Service Associates
(CASA), excavated 11 of these sites, including portions of 5LP 236,
which Homer Root had excavated in 1969. These sites were dated to
the Basketmaker II and Basketmaker III–Pueblo I periods.

Most recently, studies in Ridges Basin have been conducted under
the leadership of Francis E. Smiley of Northern Arizona University as
part of the federally funded Animas–La Plata Project. Although these
studies have been hampered by irregular funding as the project itself
has come under congressional scrutiny, Smiley's work is a very important contribution not only to Ridges Basin and Durango archaeology
but also to archaeology in the northern portion of the U.S. Southwest
in general. Smiley and his students and colleagues have shown, among
other things, that most of the Basketmaker-Pueblo sites were occupied
between A.D. 750 and 825. After this date, occupation of the basin
was very limited.

BLUE MESA

Blue Mesa is the old name, now fallen into disuse, for a Pleistocene terrace south of Durango that today is partly covered by the
Animas Air Park, light industrial development, and a small housing
subdivision. The "mesa" is about 100 meters above the Animas River
valley.

The first archaeological work on Blue Mesa was done by Harold
Gladwin in the 1930s. He recorded a large cluster of Basketmaker III
pithouses and excavated one of the larger of these. The collection of
vessels he recovered, totaling 600, is located at the University of Arizona. No more recorded work was done on the mesa until John Ives
and his archaeological field school surveyed and excavated a series of
sites. In 1974, Ives excavated a late Basketmaker III pithouse and 5
associated rooms. A year later, he supervised one of his students, Barry
Hibbetts (who went on to a professional career in archaeology), in the
excavation of another pithouse complex on the mesa. The pithouse

had been remodeled, as had the roomblock. Hibbetts completed his study of the mesa with a comprehensive survey of the mesa top that uncovered 46 sites, most of which were contemporary with the pithouses.

More detailed work continued in 1980 with the excavation of two pithouses by crews directed by Linda Honeycutt and Jerry Fetterman, who now own Woods Canyon Archaeological Consultants. These excavations were part of the archaeological work aimed at mitigating the impact of the construction of a large interstate gas pipeline. The pithouses were dated to the late eighth and early ninth centuries.

In 1983, Philip Duke and the Fort Lewis College field school excavated 5LP 1380, a small pithouse at the south end of the mesa. The pithouse was radiocarbon-dated to the early part of the seventh century.

BODO INDUSTRIAL PARK

Durango Industrial Development Foundation (DIDF), which controls Bodo Industrial Park, has been aware of the research and cultural value of the archaeological resources under its proprietorship since the 1970s. As a result, DIDF encouraged Fort Lewis College to conduct archaeological field schools on several of these properties during the late 1970s and early 1980s.

In 1974, a Fort Lewis College crew led by Susan Riches discovered 25 sites and 30 isolated finds. Four of these were later excavated by the college under the direction of Riches and Hibbetts, prior to their destruction by building construction. Sites 5LP110 and 5LP111 were excavated by John D. Gooding, archaeologist for the Colorado State Highway Department, prior to the expansion of Highway 550. In 1994, DIDF hired Mona Charles, a research associate at Fort Lewis College, to begin a site inventory and limited excavation of various archaeological sites. Her work, ongoing in 1999, has already yielded a more detailed picture of the habitation and abandonment of the populace that once occupied Bodo Industrial Park.

COLLEGE MESA AND THE SOUTHERN END OF DURANGO

The first archaeological work on College Mesa, a huge terrace on the east side of Durango, was done by Zeke Flora and Helen Sloan Daniels in the 1930s. Back then, the northern part of the mesa was referred to as Reservoir Hill. Durango's first airport was constructed on this mesa, as was the Civilian Conservation Corps camp in the 1930s. Today, Fort Lewis College, the Hillcrest Golf Course, and two housing subdivisions are located there. Anyone who spends a lot of time in ￵he rough during a game at Hillcrest will come across lithic debitage and the occasional pottery sherd.

Flora excavated Ignacio 12:23, a pithouse and roomblock complex at the north end of the mesa, in 1935. The following year, Daniels conducted more intensive investigations there. One burial was recovered. The tree-ring dates for this site are ambiguous, placing it somewhere between A.D. 430 and 670.

In the 1970s, Susan Riches and her students surveyed portions of the college campus and recovered stone flakes and ceramics. Riches later excavated a Basketmaker III pithouse (5LP 135) on the north end of the college campus, which was tree-ring-dated to the sixth century. Additionally, Anasazi ceramics and burial fragments have been found along the rim road on the west edge of the mesa.

In 1985, Gary Matlock, then of the Four Corners Research Institute of Durango, surveyed several locations near Durango that were proposed for a new landfill. Four sites of the late Basketmaker III and early Pueblo I periods were located just east of Fort Lewis College at the head of Horse Gulch, a narrow valley that widens to form a flat, fertile valley suitable for farming.

Another large concentration of Anasazi sites is located near the mouth of Horse Gulch, where it joins the Florida River. This area was surveyed by Zeke Flora. It is probable that Flora excavated in the area because he nearly always excavated any sites that he found, but no records of these excavations are known to exist. (If he did extract material from this location, it may be housed in the collections at the University of Arizona.) He also noted several other sites along Horse Gulch near the center of the small valley. Unfortunately, little is known of these sites, as most of them are on private land.

CRESTVIEW

In 1938, Helen Sloan Daniels excavated a series of sites in Crestview, then called Griffiths Heights, on the western edge of town. One site, Ignacio 12:1, a pithouse, had first been trenched by Zeke Flora in 1934 for tree-ring-dating specimens, and in fact, this was the first site to provide datable wood in Durango. Daniels's excavations were supervised by Frank Lee, a graduate of Durango High School and a sophomore at the University of Colorado at the time.

The site suffered an ignominious end. Daniels left it open for public visits, but it was ransacked by pothunters. Her plans to cover it with a permanent shelter were thwarted by the site's new owner, who could not be convinced, in Daniels's words, "of the necessity of preserving antiquities." This site is probably very close to present-day Delwood Circle. In 1989, Jill Seyfarth of the City Planner's Office and a small volunteer crew examined some trenches that were being cut for new house construction in Delwood Circle, but no more cultural remains turned up.

During the 1930s, other adjacent sites were excavated, but little information on them is available. Frank Lee excavated two more pithouses dating to the seventh century (Ignacio 12:58 and 12:59). Daniels described the most complete pottery and stone tools she found in the area, but her descriptions of the sites themselves are incomplete. She also referred in her writings to a human skull found during the excavation of a cellar south of Animas City School.

An unknown number of Anasazi sites were destroyed by the construction of the city water tower that now overlooks Junction Creek Road. Residents of the area have told us that, as children, they picked up pottery and arrowheads from that area prior to its destruction.

MISCELLANEOUS SITES

Helen Sloan Daniels excavated Ignacio 12:18 at the southern end of what is now the Riverview subdivision, prior to its destruction by gravel-extraction activities. The site comprised the remains of a roomblock and a number of burials. She also excavated what she described as a burial mound (undoubtedly a roomblock) on Logan's Farm, just south of Trimble Hot Springs, in 1936, and Zeke Flora excavated a burned pithouse (Ignacio 12:27) about 2 miles south of town on the east bank of the Animas (probably close to where Sawmill Road is today).

One final site worth mentioning is a pithouse located next to the residence of Donald Gordon, an anthropologist at Fort Lewis College, on North Bennet Drive. This site, 5LP 1859, was found during the construction of a greenhouse adjacent to Gordon's home. Interestingly, his previous residence, also at the north end of the city but on the east side of the Animas River, also had a large amount of Anasazi material on its grounds.

Anasazi material is still being turned up. Jill Seyfarth, who, as mentioned, works for the City Planner's Office, now examines many of the construction projects in Durango and, following the city's archaeological protection ordinance, records any archaeological material that she finds. In 1987, for example, a burial associated with Pueblo I artifacts was uncovered in the county fairgrounds. The material was duly turned over to local tribal representatives and reinterred in a safe place.

Since the mid-1990s, construction crews have also unearthed small archaeological finds, nearly all of them belonging to the Basketmaker-Puebloan period of occupation. When human remains have been found, Fort Lewis College archaeologist Susan Riches, who also serves as the county's deputy coroner, has worked with local Native American tribes to ensure that the remains are correctly treated.

PREHISTORIC SUBSISTENCE AND SETTLEMENT IN THE DURANGO AREA

Archaeologists use the term *settlement pattern* to describe the locations where people lived. It helps, in a general way, to understand why people chose to live in certain locations and what factors were associated with those choices. Usually, their choices had to do with the terrain and natural resources of a given locale. But, as noted earlier, there are insufficient data on Paleoindian and Archaic sites in the Durango area to permit any meaningful statements on settlement patterns during that period, although we can reasonably hypothesize that the river valley served as a major communication corridor for hunters and gatherers moving between the lower and higher elevations as the seasons changed.

The greater amount of data available for the Basketmaker III and Pueblo I periods makes inferences on their settlement patterns more feasible. For instance, we know that the settlement patterns of Basketmaker II sites were different from the Basketmaker III and Pueblo I patterns. Basketmaker II sites were located in higher elevations, well above the river valley (although Talus Village may be an exception in this regard). Basketmaker II people also appear to have relied on hunting and gathering as much as on their farming efforts, although the importance of farming may, in the past, have been underestimated by archaeologists. Perhaps it was more useful for Basketmaker II peoples to live along the boundary of the mountains and the valley to get optimal access to both environments.

Recent radiocarbon dates from corn recovered originally from the Falls Creek sites by Flora and reported by Florence Lister in her recent book on these sites are as early as the fourth century B.C. It is still difficult to assess the importance of this food item in the overall Basketmaker II diet, but it is likely that corn provided only a small portion of the peoples' intake.

During the Basketmaker period, there is also evidence that the area was intermittently abandoned, presumably in response to short-term climatic deterioration. Indeed, Michael Berry, a student of John Ives's, proposed in his doctoral dissertation that the prehistory of the northern Southwest could be partially explained as a series of population movements in and out of environmental refugia (locations in which people could take refuge from deleterious environmental conditions elsewhere) in response to changing climatic conditions. The Upper Animas served as one such refugium, and it, too, was sporadically abandoned for better areas at certain times in the past. Francis Smiley and Susan Gregg of Northern Arizona University see these periods of occupation and abandonment as a normal response to climatic fluctuations throughout the northern Southwest. Smiley makes the strong point that these short periods of occupation can be very useful to the archaeologist because they provide "snapshots" of ancient lifestyles.

During the Basketmaker III period, the Durango area supported a substantial population. Indeed, John Ware has estimated that hundreds of pithouses were built in that period. Thus, even if all of them were not inhabited at the same time, the human population must have been in the thousands. Basketmaker III peoples lived both in clusters of houses and single homesteads.

Thanks to the work in Ridges Basin, archaeologists have a fairly good idea of the range of Basketmaker sites in the Durango area. Small scatters of ceramics or lithics are the remains of specialized activities— a site where a set of tools were flaked, perhaps, or an overnight hunting spot. It is also possible that not all pithouses and roomblocks were used as primary habitation units. For example, in Ridges Basin, the large pithouses that Root dug all sat on higher-elevation ridges, which offered good vantage points for overlooking the surrounding areas as well as better soil drainage. Pithouses were also located on the alluvial fan on the basin's eastern edge, which has the most fertile soil in the basin. It is possible that the Anasazi had large fields on the fan and that the sites there had a different function than the larger units on the ridges themselves. Perhaps the fan pithouses were, in fact, field houses, used only during the growing season.

It is also interesting that Durango's Basketmaker III sites are located farther away from the Animas than might be expected. We think there are several reasons for this. First, a pithouse dug near the river could be very close to the water table, something that we presume ancient peoples would have avoided. Second, it is possible that the lands nearer to the water were among the primary farming areas and that use of these lands for houses would not make sense. Third, because the Animas valley suffers from a frost-hollow, or temperature-inversion, effect (which means that in the winter, colder air gets trapped in the bottom of the valley) it would be more comfortable living slightly higher up. Fourth, living on the higher terraces would give inhabitants a better view of and access to the surrounding countryside, and the soil would drain better; small streams cross these terraces, so carrying water up from the Animas would not have been the inhabitants' only option. Of course, it is also possible that there are sites in the flood plain that have been covered by sediments left from the regular flooding by the river. It would be necessary to excavate very deeply to locate such remains.

Although corn was an important part of the Basketmaker III and Pueblo I diet, it is likely that hunting and gathering was still a significant activity in these periods. Animals could be hunted in the surrounding forests, and everything from elk to small rabbits would have been attracted during winter to the stubble in the fields, where they could have been hunted conveniently.

The environment of Durango is normally not very conducive to intensive corn growing because corn needs about 120 frost-free days per year for good maturation and Durango's growing season is usually too short. So growing corn as a staple item must have been possible only under certain conditions. But during the eighth century, adequate climatic conditions for growing corn did exist sporadically. There is evidence for higher annual temperatures during that century, particularly at its beginning and end, and this climatic change must have increased the average number of frost-free days per year. At the same time, Durango's proximity to the mountains presumably ensured a higher level of rainfall than in places to the south. And so perhaps, if only briefly, Durango was able to sustain a heavier than normal farming economy. There is some indication that there was an increase in building activity in the latter half of the eighth century. Moreover, because of its local environment, the Durango area may have escaped the severity of many regional droughts. So, during the second half of the eighth century, the Upper Animas valley served as a refugium from drier areas: people moved in to escape the drought conditions elsewhere. At the same time, the hotter and drier conditions may have temporarily improved the agricultural potential of the Upper Animas by increasing the number of frost-free days without severely limiting precipitation. This would have further increased the area's attractiveness to farmers.

However, as the drought intensified, the lack of precipitation had more serious implications. Conditions reached such proportions at the beginning of the ninth century that some type of cultural readaptation would have been needed. Stress between the land's carrying capacity and the population levels would only have been exacerbated by the recent influx of people into the area.

In this scenario, the responses that Durango residents could have made were limited. Given existing drought conditions, switching to a greater reliance on farming would hardly have been a feasible alternative. If the population was abnormally high, as research suggests, reverting to hunting and gathering would also be unlikely because the environment could not have supported those activities. But it is possible that as agricultural systems began to fail, some emigration from the area would have occurred as a radical means of reducing population levels. Such a move would lower population levels without necessitating a full-scale abandonment of the area. Remaining groups may then have subsisted either on a greatly scaled down farming strategy or by hunting and gathering. Although there is little evidence for this third scenario, it should be pointed out that the majority of sites in the Durango area were originally located by amateurs who were primarily interested in locating large pithouse sites. The more ephemeral remains of hunters and gatherers were beyond their interest.

Mona Charles's careful excavations of sites in Bodo suggest that the abandonment of the area, if it actually happened, might not have been quick and absolute. Rather, she suggests that casual abandonment and possibly relocation to a new pithouse at the same site or a nearby location were not uncommon. All pithouses appear to have been inhabited during the same general time period, but they were not necessarily inhabited precisely contemporaneously. Trash-filled pithouses and postoccupational hearths suggest that such houses and hearths were reused for an undetermined time after their initial abandonment. Charles's work compels archaeologists to develop much more precise abandonment models for the Durango area.

However, we do want to stress that our reconstruction of settlement and subsistence patterns is still largely conjectural. Archaeologists need to conduct many more detailed studies of past environments in Durango and of the specific human responses to environmental change before they can speak with any certainty about how the environment determined human behavior in Durango's prehistoric past.

The Ute and the Navajo

There is no clear archaeological evidence to establish when the Ute first appeared in the Durango area, although linguistic evidence suggests that it is at least possible that they arrived sometime in the last thousand years. The Navajo also used the valley at a later point.

Unfortunately, archaeologists have a great deal of difficulty in recognizing either the Ute or the Navajo in the archaeological record. Although plenty of projectile points and other artifacts ranging back as far as 5,000 or 6,000 years have been found in mountain sites near Durango, it is unclear whether these Archaic sites are the remains of the ancestors of the Ute. Part of the problem is that hunting-and-gathering peoples are generally mobile and leave little behind in the way of housing, campsites, tools, and other durable artifacts. And because many of the early peoples' daily containers and articles of clothing were made from plants—woven baskets and similar objects—most items of this type would not have lasted long.

Unless we find some very distinctive artifact that can be consistently and uniquely tied to either the Ute or Navajo people, it will be impossible to trace these groups back in the archaeological record much beyond the historical written record of the more recent Europeans. Of course, both of those tribes have their own histories describing when and how they came into the area, and we must not denigrate these simply because they are not like a European version of history. Still, it would be satisfying to have an archaeological history of the Ute and the Navajo that could connect the people of today with past cultural remains.

THE UTE

The Ute are the great mountain peoples of the West. When Spanish explorers and traders initially entered the Animas valley, the first Native Americans they met were the Ute, and it was the Ute who would serve as guides to the Spanish explorers of the eighteenth century. Historical accounts of the early European settlers, of miners, and of cowboys alike consistently note encounters with these people.

Today, the Ute are the only Native American tribe with reservations in Colorado. In southwestern Colorado, the Southern Ute reservation, composed of the Capote and Mouache bands, is centered on the town of Ignacio, about 15 miles south of Durango; the Ute Mountain Ute, comprised primarily of the Weeminuche band, are centered around Towaoc, south of Cortez.

Prior to being placed on reservations in the nineteenth century, the tribe had occupied around 130,000 square miles of territory, extending from west-central Utah to the plains of Colorado and including a strip running along the northern edge of New Mexico to the San Juan River in the area south of Mesa Verde. In Colorado, their original territory—56 million acres—was reduced to 18 million acres by 1868. By 1934, the Southern Utes were reduced by 99 percent to 40,600 acres, and in the same period, the Ute Mountain reservation was down by 94 percent to 513,000 acres. Since 1934, the tribes have purchased additional tracts of land, so that by 1996, the Southern Ute reservation encompassed approximately 432,000 acres and the Ute Mountain Ute reservation covered 530,000 acres.

The Ute probably immigrated from the west. Their culture is basically Great Basin in origin with an overlay of more recent Plains culture traits, although at least one living Ute elder believes that the Capote and Mouache traditionally arrived from the east. Eastern Ute

47

bands had contacted the Spanish by the first part of the seven-
teenth century and thereby acquired horses and some elements of
the Plains Indian lifestyle. Seventeenth- and eighteenth-century raids
into New Mexico, for the purpose of stealing horses from the Spanish and other goods from the Pueblo people, also contributed to
the eclecticism that characterizes much Ute culture.

Residence groups numbered from 50 to 100 people, with larger
accumulations possible in the summer. Bands were composed of several residence units, led by a headman who consulted with a council
made up of the other residence unit leaders.

Prior to the reservation period, the Ute were generalized hunters
and gatherers. They hunted deer, elk, antelope, bison (on the Eastern
Slope and on the plains), rabbit, birds, ground squirrels, waterfowl,
crickets, and cicadas. They also caught fish, although this resource
was more important to the western bands. The Ute gathered sunflower
seeds, grass seeds, cactus blossoms, fruit, roots, tubers, berries, and
thistles, as well as wild tobacco. The Weeminuche may also have grown
some corn. Women were the primary gatherers, although men might
have helped with the piñon nut harvest, combining this activity with
the fall deer hunting.

In southern Colorado, seasonal movements were primarily altitu-
dinal, with bands moving into present-day northern New Mexico for
the winter. The specific routes they followed, however, are not known.
A description of a Historic Ute encampment was provided by J. S.
Newberry, a geologist on the Macomb Expedition. On July 30, 1859,
Newberry visited the camp of Sobertah, located about 12 miles west of
present-day Pagosa Springs. Even so early in the year, the Ute were
apparently preparing for winter: "[they were] collecting and drying
[service] berries," Newberry recorded, and there were "squaws dressing
and painting [?] skins."

Traditional Ute technologies included leatherwork, basketry,
woodwork, and cordage. Their stone-tool technology included arrow
points, scrapers, drills, round or oval manos, and both thin-slab and
deep-trough metates. The Eastern Ute groups did not make pottery at
all, but some Weeminuche made coiled pottery. Although pottery
does not appear to have been an important technology during the
Historic period, perhaps it was more important during the Prehistoric
period; certainly, pottery items were among the first to be abandoned

in favor of European goods by many aboriginal hunting-and-gathering groups.

Ute living structures included tripod or conical houses called *wickiups*. Ute wickiups were about 15 feet in diameter and 8 feet high and were covered with willows, juniper bark, and grass. These traditional lodges were later replaced by Plains tipis as the tribe fell under the influence of Plains culture during the nineteenth century. Wickiup-type sweathouses were also constructed; only Eastern Ute bands used the conical type. A sweathouse was heated by rocks carried in from the outside.

The Ute language is one of two assigned to the Southern Numic branch of the Uto-Aztecan language family, the other being Kawaiisu. The original Numic speakers were Archaic-stage peoples who lived in and around the Great Basin before migrating in a number of directions (in the so-called Numic Expansion) and undergoing further linguistic and social divergence. Linguists have argued that the Numic language originated in the southwest corner of the Great Basin and that the split into the three Numic branches—Western, Central, and Southern—occurred sometime around 2,000 years ago. The expansion northward and eastward is thought to have taken place about 1,000 years ago, and it is this movement that brought the Ute into Colorado. However, as with almost any subject of scholarship, there is disagreement about this issue. Some archaeologists and linguists believe that the Ute as a separate ethnic group have been in Colorado for several thousand years. If this is true, it will force archaeologists to thoroughly revise southwest Colorado's prehistory.

As mentioned earlier, it has been very difficult for archaeologists to identify a specific Ute artifact assemblage or site. They have tried to isolate particular projectile point types, ceramic technologies, and house styles, among others facets of the culture, but all of these seem to have been used by other groups, too. More depressing still to the archaeologist is the fact that it is also possible that tribes signaled their ethnic distinctiveness with material culture that has not survived into the archaeological record. And most depressing of all is the possibility that these tribes may have had no ethnically distinct material culture at all.

Nonetheless, some sites in the vicinity of Durango may well have been Ute, even if we cannot establish this identity through the archaeological record. For instance, south of town, Jeffrey Wharton and Walt Heikes (the latter is still active in local preservation issues) excavated a four-pole, forked-stick structure as part of a Fort Lewis College project, under the direction of Robert W. "Bill" Biggs. This site, dated by architectural type and associated pottery to A.D. 1775–1875, comprises four standing poles, possibly another eighteen fallen poles, two fallen pole sockets or abutments, a hearth, a small cist, a grinding slab, and assorted lithic and ceramic fragments.

The remains of a Ute-period brush shelter (structure #5) have been found at Talus Village, probably built between A.D. 1600 and 1774. The structure differs from the nearby Basketmaker II structural remains in several respects: it is oval in shape, it has no subfloor cists, it apparently had a different roofing system, and it lacks the artifact assemblage of the earlier structures. Its identification as a Ute shelter is based as much on the *lack* of definite evidence that it is Puebloan, Navajo, or Apache as on positive evidence that it is Ute.

Also of probable Ute origin are "scarred" Ponderosa pine trees like those depicted in Figure 3.10. The scars were created by the removal of phloem and cambium cells (inner bark) for human utilization and consumption, which was first noted by Meriwether Lewis and William Clark in 1805. Marilyn Martorano, who studied inner-bark consumption by the Ute for her master's thesis at Colorado State University, concluded that the Ute people used bark as a food supplement in periods of dietary stress. Martorano dated the majority of scarred trees in Colorado to between 1815 and 1875, a date that is consistent with the bark's use as a "stress food" because during this period, the Ute were being pushed from their traditional territory under the onslaught of Euroamerican invasion.

THE NAVAJO

The Navajo make up the largest group of Native Americans in the United States. Today, they live on a reservation that is as large as many states, and they occupy a substantial section of the Four Corners area. The Navajo number approximately 140,000 individuals (from a low of 15,000 in 1868) and control a reservation about 16 million acres in size. They speak a variation of Southern Athabascan and are related linguistically and culturally to the Apache. The Navajo were originally hunters and gatherers, but after coming into

3.10 Scarred Ponderosa pine. Probably dating to the end of the nineteenth century, the scar was made by the removal of the exterior bark to get at the edible inner bark.

contact with the Spanish, they also began sheepherding, a practice they still rely on today. The Navajo culture is considered to be a classic example of cultural syncretism, in that today it incorporates elements borrowed from the Spanish, the Anglos, and neighboring Puebloan groups.

It was the Spanish who first noted the close cultural and linguistic affinities between the Navajo and the Apache. Language similarities in particular have led linguists to conclude that both groups arrived relatively recently in the American Southwest from the north and split apart after their arrival. The logic of this interpretation derives from the fact that both groups have close linguistic neighbors in central Alaska and Canada. By using a technique called "glotto-chronology," which determines how long ago linguistically related peoples separated from one another, most Western scholars have concluded that the Navajo arrived in the Southwest shortly before the Spanish, although just how much before is still unclear.

Indigenous oral tradition and archaeological and linguistic interpretation do not always agree about just when the Navajo arrived in the Southwest. Many Navajo, for instance, believe their people have been in the area *forever*, and though archaeologists do not share this view, they *are* constantly finding new evidence that the Navajo existed in the Southwest earlier than prior archeological research suggested.

The earliest archaeological evidence of a Navajo presence perhaps does not include pottery but does include side-notched projectile points used with the bow and arrow, conical habitation structures, and twined and flat-coiled basketry. Historic accounts suggest these Navajo were a hunting-and-gathering, maize-growing people who traded with Puebloan people and probably exploited the resources of the San Juan Mountains. It is likely, given their probable northern origins, that they arrived in the Southwest with a generalized hunting-and-gathering assemblage that included the sinew-backed bow and perhaps pottery. Their original house structure was a forked-stick hogan, later replaced by the more substantially constructed cribbed-dome hogan that is still used on the reservation today.

As mentioned, recent archaeological research is gradually pushing the date of the Navajo occupation of the Four Corners area even further back. Until a few years ago, archaeological evidence indicated that the Navajo arrived only slightly before the Spanish, moving in from the east about the time of the Pueblo Revolt of 1680 and living at first in the Gobernador area of New Mexico and the Jemez Mountains in mutual communities with Pueblo exiles—the so-called *Pueblito* occupation.

Sites that have been identified as Navajo have been dated by
tree rings at least as early as 1600, and there are Navajo sites south
of Durango along the New Mexico border that date from that time
to well into the 1700s. Rock art in the same area is also attributed
to the Navajo. However, new research suggests that the Navajo's
arrival could have been much earlier; perhaps as early as the late
A.D. 1300s. It is possible that further investigation will show Navajo
occupation overlapping with that of the Ancestral Pueblo.

Some Navajo sites have been found in the southern part of La
Plata County. U.S. Forest Service surveys in the high mountains have
located one Navajo site west of the La Plata Mountains; the site dates
to around A.D. 1680. However, beyond these few pieces of evidence,
we have little reason thus far to believe that Navajo people ever had
much of a permanent presence in the Durango area or the Animas
River valley. This is somewhat surprising because the La Plata Mountains are among the four world-defining mountain peaks of the Navajo world (the other three being the San Francisco Peaks, Mount
Taylor, and Navajo Mountain).

The Archaeology of Euroamerican Durango

Permanent European settlement of the Durango area occurred in
the late nineteenth century. Durango, founded by the Denver and
Rio Grande Railroad in 1880 as the terminus of the route from Denver and as a railhead and shipping point for mining products and
supplies, quickly became the primary economic center for the region.
Coal mining, which was especially important between 1872 and 1945,
depended first on the development of tollroads and then on the railroads. The La Plata coalfield that runs through La Plata, Montezuma,
Dolores, and San Miguel Counties was developed to power the ore
smelters.

Railroads in this region, the final sign of the area's entry into the
industrial world, were built primarily to carry ores and timber to pro-
cessing centers. Their impact on settlement were far-reaching. For
instance, the Denver and Rio Grande builders had intended that
Animas City would be the center of their rail operation, but when the
town failed to grant the demanded concessions, the railroad bought
land and built a company town nearby, a town that they could
control. That town was Durango, established in September 1880,

and it quickly became populated at the expense of Animas City's demise. It also became the site of the San Juan and New York smelters.

Probably the most extensive information on historical sites in the area is in the surveys conducted by the U.S. Forest Service, the Bureau of Land Management, and consultant archaeologists working for companies building the pipelines, oil fields, and roads around Durango. Unfortunately, almost none of this information is readily available to the public. Instead, the sites are tightly guarded by federal managers to prevent bottle hunters and looters from damaging these locations. Consequently, although the information and, to some extent, the sites themselves are safer, little archaeological knowledge of this period is accessible to the public.

In 1983, archaeologists Gary Matlock and Jon Horn, of Nickens and Associates, excavated a small cabin site on lands that Tamarron Resort proposed to exchange with the U.S. Forest Service. Tamarron paid for the research. The cabin was a small, single-room log structure that stood along the wagon road between Durango and the mining town of Silverton. This road, called the Animas City–Silverton Wagon Road, preceded the narrow-gauge railroad and was the main route for moving material and people between the two towns from 1876 to 1881. Tree-ring dates from wood near the cabin's fireplace document that it was built in 1878. It likely functioned as a toll cabin at which fees were collected from freighters and travelers along the roadway.

The cabin and the surrounding area yielded a huge number and variety of cartridges from guns ranging from small derringer-type pistols to large 90-caliber buffalo rifles. Why there was so much shooting around the cabin is unknown, but one can't help but wonder if some of the gunslinging scenes portrayed in Western movies were not, indeed, enacted at the cabin.

Within the town of Durango itself, a number of historical archaeology studies have also been done. Unfortunately, all of them were products of "hurry-up" archaeology completed just before construction was to begin. In 1984, a volunteer crew of students and local amateur archaeologists led by Philip Duke excavated a historical site prior to the construction of the Red Lion Inn (now the Doubletree Hotel), the first project completed under the city's archaeological protection policy. This location had been the site of a lumber mill founded by relatives of Helen Sloan Daniels. It then became a hard-

3.11 Historic period sewer system, Doubletree Hotel.

ware store and a flour mill run by the Graden family. At the north end of the site was a slaughterhouse. Most of the buildings were wood, and many had regularly burned down, which probably explains the heavy deposits of charcoal, slag, and burned soil that were excavated.

Of most interest was the excavation of a series of shaped slabs of stone, each one approximately 1 meter long and 50 centimeters wide (Figure 3.11). Cut into the surface of each, across the long axis, was a groove about 30 centimeters wide and 10 centimeters deep. In consultation with local historian Duane Smith of Fort Lewis College, the archaeologists decided that this was part of a very rudimentary open sewer system, taking waste material from the south end of Main Avenue directly into the Animas River.

In 1985, the La Plata County Courthouse was expanded with an addition on the south of the old building. At the last minute, the city officials realized that the basement of the new addition was to be constructed over the old Durango jail. Although archaeologists from Fort Lewis College were able to conduct only a couple of days of excavations and examination (construction for the new basement was already under way before the archaeologists were notified), they did find substantial remains of the original basement jail that housed Durango's worst citizens. Fragments of a cement floor, metal bar attachments, remains of early plumbing, and other articles were found. With so little time to work, however, the archaeological team could not learn much, and no real documentation of the early jail was possible. Ultimately, all or most of what was there was destroyed by the construction of the new courthouse.

Yet beneath the current homes and businesses in Durango lie a wealth of undiscovered structural remains of a nineteenth-century Victorian town. To date, a number of intriguing finds have been made. A wine cellar was found behind the Strater Hotel, and old foundations, pit toilets, streets, and other materials are routinely encountered during building construction. In 1990, workers laying a water line uncovered the remains of the original oak-stave water line that ran up to the city reservoir. Hitching rings are regularly found in old Durango whenever new sidewalks are laid. And in 1992, during new construction of shops at the corner of 14th and Main, the remains of a brewing or bottling establishment were uncovered.

The Horse Gulch survey conducted by Gary Matlock also located one of the oldest trash dumps in Durango, one that has been largely forgotten by current residents of the city. During the survey, archaeologists discovered an enterprising Fort Lewis student excavating the remains of a 1930s automobile in hopes of selling the parts and helping to pay his way though school. The trash dump is an excellent example of an important European archaeological site that should be preserved, for as most people recognize, such a site can provide a chronological sequence of the physical remains of Durango's early-twentieth-century history.

We hope that as Durango matures, its citizens will learn to appreciate these more recent remains of the city's fascinating western past. One thing is certain: if they fail to do so, most of these irreplaceable treasures will soon be gone forever.

4
A History of Durango Archaeology

This chapter is devoted to the history of archaeology in Durango and to the dedicated amateurs who put Durango on the world archaeological map. However, the story of Durango's archeological past can only be properly understood if it is told within the wider context of world archaeology and the archaeology of the American Southwest.

Archaeology as a scientific discipline has two distinct intellectual roots, both of them originating in Europe. The first stems from the eighteenth-century interest in the antiquities of Greece and Rome. In that era, rich young men from France and England were sent on "Grand Tours" of Greece and Italy to immerse themselves in the high culture of these ancient civilizations: beautiful pottery, sculpture, art, and architecture. Throughout the succeeding century, classical archaeologists, as they came to be known, revealed the origins of ancient civilizations, in both the Old and New Worlds. A premium was placed on locating beautiful objects that could be displayed in museums.

The second intellectual root grew out of the nineteenth-century development of the "hard" sciences of biology and geology. Charles Darwin's theory of evolution, published in 1859, held that all organisms were engaged in a constant struggle for survival that led to increasingly well-adapted forms of life. Archaeologists, like their colleagues in the related discipline of anthropology, borrowed this model as a means of explaining changes in human societies over time. Indeed, it was thought that all societies would pass through the same stages of cultural evolution, from "savagery" through "barbarism" to "civilization." Unfortunately, although there is nothing inherently racist about evolutionary theory when applied to biology, its application in explaining why human societies changed through time *was* racist because it implied that it is natural for certain societies or races to dominate others.

It would be many years before the unsuitability of this model for explaining *cultural* change was finally realized. The demise of this simplistic evolutionary model is largely attributable to the work of the father of American anthropology, Franz Boas, who emigrated to the United States from Germany in the late nineteenth century. (Boas's work may have been shaped, in part, by his own experiences with anti-Semitism at the American universities where he taught for many years.) Today, archaeologists have abandoned the simplistic and racist notions of the nineteenth century. However, the idea that societies change in order to adapt to a dynamic environment is still respected.

Geology, the study of the earth, offered archaeologists a means of dating archaeological sites. Nineteenth-century geologists invented the concept of the "type fossil," whereby a particular geological stratum could be dated by identifying a fossil within the layer that was unique to a specific period. Then, if another stratum somewhere else also had that unique fossil, the geologists could conclude that the two strata were contemporary. Archaeologists borrowed this concept and organized the past into distinct periods and cultures, each of which was distinguished by a few diagnostic (i.e., unique) artifacts.

During the first 50 years of the twentieth century, archaeologists, especially those in America, were concerned with organizing their data into what are still called space-time frameworks, in effect pigeonholing sites and artifacts so that they could be dated. (We say "especially those in America" because European archaeologists erroneously thought that they had accurately dated their prehistoric sites simply by comparing them to the dated historical civilizations of the eastern Mediterranean. The development of radiocarbon dating in the late 1940s showed them the error of their ways, but that's another story entirely.) So, the first of half of this century witnessed the appearance of the first major theoretical approach to archaeology—*culture history*, which attempted to answer the questions of what, who, when, and where.

In 1949, archaeology was transformed by the invention of radiocarbon dating. This technique allowed archaeologists anywhere in the world to date organic remains from their sites accurately and efficiently. No longer did they have to spend most of their time estimating the age of a site. Now, they could date it quickly and turn their attention to other pressing questions.

In North America, the research questions that archaeologists focused on involved the relationship of past cultures to the environment (in this regard, they played catch-up with European archaeologists, who had been looking at these questions for at least 30 years). Archaeologists began to study why sites were located in particular places and how past societies exploited the natural setting.

At the same time, an iconoclastic young archaeologist, Walter Taylor, published a revolutionary book that lambasted the traditional way of doing American archaeology. He wrote that archaeology had become obsessed with the study of artifacts rather than with the people who made them. He advocated a radical departure from the status quo, arguing that archaeologists should try to *understand* past human behavior, not simply analyze artifacts in the process of constructing a culture history of an area.

Taylor's work hit a raw nerve with many of the older generation. Further, Taylor made the impolitic move of criticizing the grand old man of American archaeology, the southwesternist Alfred Kidder. Taylor's work was pompously dismissed. However, it is impossible to keep a good idea down forever, and Taylor's work eventually became one of the inspirations behind the second great theoretical approach to archaeology—*processualism*.

Processual archaeology was founded by Lewis Binford, an angry young archaeologist who, with an ardent band of disciples, turned his field on its head throughout the 1960s. He and his associates argued that archaeology should become a hard science—developing hypotheses, testing them statistically, and formulating laws of human behavior. They rejected virtually all the tenets of culture history. Today, processual archaeology is still a major approach in the field. Indeed, elements of it have become so commonplace that many archaeologists do not even realize they are doing processual work; for them, archaeology has *always* been done this way.

However, archaeology never stands still, and processual archaeology is now being threatened by the rise of a new theoretical approach called *postprocessualism*. This approach encompasses a number of contemporary social and political trends. For example, it embraces a much greater commitment to feminist studies in archaeology. It also tries to accommodate Native American versions of the past and address the issue of who actually "owns" the past (if anyone does). Postprocessual archaeologists do not claim that archaeology is a hard science, preferring instead to consider it more like history—a field in which different interpretations of the data can be accepted as equally legitimate and valid. Perhaps most important of all, postprocessualism emphasizes that the past is a creation of the present in that the types of questions we want answered about the past determine how our descriptions of that past are formed; put another way, how we interpret the past is determined by the present, and the present is, in part, determined by the past.

Throughout all these heady theoretical changes, the role of the amateur archaeologist has continued to be of paramount importance. In almost every area of the world where archaeology is practiced, the first interest in the past of an area has been shown by amateurs. Though not professionally trained, many of these individuals have acquired an amazing depth of knowledge because of their familiarity with the sites they visit. Indeed, amateur archaeologists have often paved the way for the professional archaeologists, leading them to sites, helping with the excavations, and, most important, putting pressure on governments to protect the archaeological finds themselves. All over the world, amateur archaeological societies flourish, and we can think of no other profession in which amateur participation has been so vital and integral to its development.

The dark side to amateur involvement is, of course, the scourge of the pothunter who destroys sites and the information they contain to obtain a few pretty pots. We have no truck with such people;

their uncontrolled and unrecorded excavations, aimed at nothing more than removing the most "valuable" (i.e., marketable) artifacts, damage archaeological sites to the point that the information they contain is often lost entirely. After all, getting this information and interpreting the site in its entirety is the sole point of a scientific excavation.

However, it does behoove professionals to ask one simple question about the pothunter who does, in fact, have an interest in the past and who is not just looking for financial gain: "what interests this person about the past, and how can legitimate professional archaeology satisfy that curiosity to draw him or her back into the wider archaeological community?"

In 1906, it was public concern over the increasing loss of archaeological sites that led to the creation of the Antiquities Act, the first U.S. law to protect such sites. Ultimately, in the 1970s, this concern spawned what is now called cultural resource management (CRM), an outgrowth of a number of federal laws requiring that all public lands be monitored for archaeological sites before any development took place on them. In other words, if sites were to be destroyed, they first had to be adequately studied by professional archaeologists. The resulting increase in the database of archaeology was phenomenal, and archaeology was able to employ many more people than ever before.

SOUTHWESTERN ARCHAEOLOGY: A BRIEF HISTORY

Nearly all of the early travelers and members of exploration parties that visited the Southwest from the sixteenth century onward commented on the highly visible ruins they encountered along the way. Early Spanish explorers such as Francisco Vasquez de Coronado, Fray Marcos de Niza, Pedro de Castenada, and Juan de Oñate described the ruins along the Rio Grande valley and correctly identified them as ancestral sites belonging to the Pueblo villages they found at Taos, Pecos, and elsewhere. In addition, participants in the two major Spanish explorations in southwestern Colorado—that of Juan Maria Antonio Rivera in 1765 and of Fray Francisco Atanasio Dominguez and Fray Silvestre Véles de Escalante in 1776—documented their explorations in diaries and noted abandoned ruins sighted during their travels.

In the 1760s, a metal-prospecting party was sent to the San Juans by the governor of New Mexico, and in 1765, the Rivera Expedition established the path of the Spanish Trail. The quasi-missionary Dominguez and Escalante Expedition in 1776 sought a trade route to California that would not be impeded by either the Hopi and Apache tribes. Following a route that took them along the southern fringes of the San Juan Mountains, the party crossed the San Juan River in the vicinity of present-day Pagosa Junction and then moved west, crossing the Piedra, Pine, Florida, and Animas Rivers in the process. The expedition crossed the Animas somewhere south of Durango, and the explorers described an open meadow that would provide good pasture for horses. This pasture, they noted, was up a tributary, west of the Animas. It sounds like Ridges Basin.

In general, the Spanish showed little interest in researching any of the ruins they found. They were far more concerned with agriculture, commerce, trading with a variety of Native American groups and peoples, and building the towns and cities of New Mexico and Arizona.

After New Mexico, Colorado, and Arizona became part of the United States in 1848, the U.S. government sent out exploration parties to describe and evaluate this new part of America. Many of these expeditions entered southwestern Colorado, the most notable being the San Juan Exploring Expedition of 1859 (also known as the Macomb Expedition), led by John Macomb and the Hayden Expedition of 1874–1876. On each of these expeditions, notes and drawing of the ruins in southwestern Colorado and the Four Corners area were made.

In 1874, some of Mesa Verde's ruins were captured by the famous photographer William Henry Jackson. A year later, William Holmes, the pioneering geologist of the San Juans, visited Mesa Verde and began to bring the area's magnificence to the public's attention through his newspaper articles and formal reports. Little substantive information that would help our understanding of the archaeology and prehistory of the area was acquired from these expeditions, but they did serve to publicize the existence of the massive prehistoric remains of the Southwest and Colorado to the nation.

As the Southwest was settled by European-Americans, its ruins began to attract interest for the same reasons that the classical civilizations of Europe had, for they contained beautiful pottery worthy of museum display and the well-preserved sites were relatively easy to uncover. Interest was shown both by the local amateurs and pothunters and by the new breed of professional archaeologists. Southwest archaeology became a marriage of these two interests, as the description of how Mesa Verde was found demonstrates. The evolution of Four Corners archaeology in particular is rooted in the "discovery" of Mesa Verde and its subsequent study.

Today, Mancos is a sleepy little town, serving the needs of the local ranching community and, in the summer, the occasional tourist. However, 100 years ago, it was the center of worldwide archaeological interest. And the people responsible for this were the legendary Wetherills.

South of the town, the Mancos River enters a deep sandstone canyon at the southern end of Mesa Verde. In the late 1800s, this land was part of the Ute Mountain Ute reservation, and because the Ute people were none too friendly to outsiders, the canyon was rarely entered by white ranchers and miners. Those who did venture into the area generally kept a low profile.

The exception to this rule was the Wetherill family. B. K. Wetherill and his five sons ran a cattle ranch to the west and a little south of town, and with the permission of the Ute, they wintered their cattle in Mancos Canyon. By 1888, the Wetherills and nearly everyone else who had gone into the canyons were aware of the many ruins in the caves and sandstone alcoves there. The ruins were generally small and made of sandstone masonry walls, and they usually contained a few fragments of pottery and other artifacts.

In the winter of 1888, Richard Wetherill, his brothers Al and Clayton and his brother-in-law Charles Mason were camped in the main Mancos Canyon, herding and gathering cattle that had strayed up into the canyons to the north. On December 8, as Richard and Charlie were riding through the dense pinon-juniper forest, they came to the edge of a canyon and looked across for the first time at Cliff Palace, a 200-room village up to 4 stories in height that had been built into a deep cave in the face of the sandstone cliff. The following day, the cowboys explored other canyons and found many other large villages similar to, although not quite as large as, Cliff Palace.

Such spectacular ruins attracted academic archaeologists to the Southwest, and universities started to send out research groups in earnest just after the turn of the twentieth century. In the first two decades of the new century, research centers were established in places such as Santa Fe, Flagstaff, Globe, and Tucson. Scholars from as far afield as Europe were attracted to these towns to study the Anasazi and other archaeological cultures, such as the Hohokam in southern Arizona and the Mogollon along the Arizona–New Mexico border. At that time, most scholars were solitary figures, usually working alone and often at some risk of being lost or perishing in the Southwest deserts or at the hand of a renegade cowboy. This sounds a little like the stuff of Indiana Jones, but we suspect that the analogy is fairly accurate.

A turning point in Southwest archaeology came in 1927 when Alfred Kidder organized the First Pecos Conference, named after the pueblo he was excavating close to Santa Fe. Kidder invited numerous southwestern archaeologists to help devise a culture-historical framework for the region. The result was the Pecos Classification, which defined three Basketmaker and five Pueblo periods.

Interestingly, the Pecos Classification is a perfect example of how the two roots of archaeology (classical archaeology, with its emphasis on fine pottery and architecture, and the hard sciences, particularly geology) became intertwined because Kidder used different pottery and architectural styles as "type fossils" for each of the phases he proposed. As a young man, Kidder had toured Greece and Italy on his own version of the Grand Tour, and it is tempting to speculate that this exposure was instrumental in his development of the Pecos system.

The Southwest's lead in American archaeology was not due to the fantastic preservation of its ruins alone, however. In the early years of the twentieth century, the astronomer A. E. Douglass had given southwestern archaeologists a jump on others in the discipline by developing the technique of tree-ring dating, a technique perfectly suited to the prehistoric cultures of the Southwest, where dry climates and the heavy use of timber in building construction gave archaeologists the opportunity to develop the world's first absolute dating technique. Douglass had begun research on this technique as early as 1904, although it was not until 1929 that the tree-ring sequence was finally linked to the absolute dates of the Christian calendar.

THE ROLE OF DURANGO IN THE DEVELOPMENT
OF SOUTHWESTERN ARCHAEOLOGY

Early Durangoans were aware of the rich historical remains that surrounded them in every direction, and farmers, travelers, prospectors, and ranchers must have regularly encountered prehistoric pottery, tumbled stone mounds, and carved rock-art designs. Durangoans no doubt speculated about the abundant Indian ruins, listened to the tales that cowboys and travelers told in the local bars and restaurants, and provided the services necessary for those exploring the Native American past.

However, beyond viewing these archaeological sites and artifacts with curiosity, the earliest Durangoans seemed much too busy to undertake serious investigation of the ruins and relics, apart from some random digging and collecting for pots and other artifacts. Indeed, few names of Durangoans are associated with the discovery, exploration, or research that was taking place in the late 1800s. Ultimately, the importance of these ruins was first appreciated in other parts of southwestern Colorado and by individuals outside the state.

Yet Durango still played a vital role in developing the region's archaeology, and local businesspeople realized that the town's railroad could serve as a key link in bringing people to visit the sites of southwestern Colorado. For example, in 1907, Kidder, then teaching at Harvard, stopped in Durango on his way to meet Edgar Hewitt and Sylvanus Morley, two other famous American archaeologists. He would not be the last archaeologist to use Durango in this way, and many other early tourists would travel to Durango by train and then rent a coach or wagon to get to Mancos and beyond. In other words, the citizens and business community of Durango may not have found Mesa Verde and its spectacular ruins, but they certainly capitalized on their popularity. Durango's role then, much as it is today, was to serve as the jumping-off point for those interested in historic sites and as the last place for these people to find good hotels, restaurants, and necessary supplies.

It was partly an interest in guarding the archaeological goose laying the golden eggs that prompted Durangoans to protect the remains of the Anasazi. In April 1893, the Durango Archaeological and Historical Society was organized to purchase pothunted collections from the Mesa Verde region and to prevent Gustav Nordenskiold from taking back to his native Sweden artifacts that he had excavated from Cliff Palace with Richard Wetherill. The Durango-Nordenskiold connection is a fascinating one, carefully retold by Duane Smith in his fascinating book on the history of Mesa Verde National Park.

Nordenskiold was 22 years old when he arrived from Sweden to tour the newly discovered ruins of Mesa Verde in 1891. Traveling from New York to Denver, he proceeded by train to Durango, and from there he took a coach to Mancos, where he was a guest of the Wetherills. After several months of digging, he loaded up his "treasures" for shipment from Durango to Sweden. Irate locals prevented the shipment from being boarded on an eastbound train, and Nordenskiold found himself slandered in the Durango and Denver newspapers. The ultimate indignity came when he was arrested and forced to post a $1,000 bond. As it turned out, there were no actual statutes to prevent Nordenskiold from shipping the artifacts, which he subsequently did, but such activity provided, in part, the stimulus that led to the creation of Mesa Verde National Park in 1906 and the passage that same year of the Antiquities Act, the first attempt to protect the country's ancient sites and artifacts.

Women played a key role in fighting for these two seminal acts. Although many citizens bemoaned the looting of Mesa Verde, it was women (often with the full support of their husbands) who actually banded together to stop it. Notable among them were Estell Camp of Durango, wife of a local banker, and Helen Stoiber of Silverton, wife of a mine owner. They worked closely with Lucy Peabody in Washington and Virginia McClurg in Denver to launch the historic preservation movement and make Mesa Verde a national park. The Colorado Federated Women's Club also began its long association with archaeology during this turbulent time. It still has an important voice, helping, for example, to establish the Anasazi Heritage Center in Dolores.

After this first spurt of interest in archaeology, the next two decades saw relatively little involvement by Durango people. Why their interest waned is unclear, but it may have been a reflection of the changes that their town experienced as it settled into the rather bourgeois community that it is today. Of course, there were still entrepreneurs, but the pioneering spirit of adventure that produced both the first archaeologists and the first towns and industries in the area had subsided.

Not until several decades later was the first documented professional research in the immediate Durango area conducted. This occurred in 1929 and was sponsored by a private research organization called Gila Pueblo, located in Globe, Arizona. The Gila Pueblo organization, financially supported and directed by the millionaire Harold S. Gladwin and his wife Winifred, was one of a number of such organizations formed during the early part of the century. Most of the Gila Pueblo's initial research centered on the nearby ruins of southern Arizona. However, in the late 1920s, the Gila Pueblo staff members decided to try to determine the exact extent and variety of southwestern cultures, in particular the Anasazi, and they sent out teams of young archaeologists in every direction to conduct basic site surveys and explorations.

One of these teams, sent to Durango in 1929, produced the first serious archaeological survey of the area. Roland K. Smith and Ted Amundsen conducted a random survey of sites, based largely on information provided by locals. Site forms were completed for each of these ruins, and although the information was fairly minimal, the survey put Durango on the archaeological map (Box 4.1). It also alerted professional archaeologists to the fact that the Animas valley, overshadowed for many decades by Mesa Verde and the spectacular ruins in the Montezuma valley, also contained significant Anasazi remains. The survey noted what was to be one of the great puzzles of Durango archaeology: why do all the sites belong to the Basketmaker III and Pueblo I periods? It was this project that brought Harold Gladwin to the area in 1935 to excavate the sites on Blue Mesa.

One of the standard procedures that the Gila Pueblo staffers

BOX 4.1
DURANGO'S SITE NUMBERING SYSTEMS

A brief word is in order on how archaeological sites in Durango are numbered. Today, American archaeologists use the Smithsonian Designation System: for example, in site number 5LP 10, the 5 refers to Colorado, the LP to La Plata County, and the 10 to the tenth site in the county that was recorded in the State Archaeologist's Office in Denver. The numbers are distributed by this office, so theoretically, no number is ever used twice. The system is used throughout the country and is easily understood.

However, things were not always so simple, and anyone who has examined the site records for Durango has run into site numbers that are quite different from those used today. Thus, some sites are described as, for example, B:9:1, CO B:9:1, Ignacio:7:101 (GP), La Plata:5:2 (GP), and so on. These site numbers are based on a system used by Gila Pueblo, which was slightly modified by Zeke Flora, Helen Sloan Daniels, and Homer Root during the 1930s and 1940s. The system finally became obsolete when the Smithsonian Designation System was introduced.

In general, the Gila system worked as follows. Gila Pueblo designated a series of topographic quad maps as areas A, B, C, etc., within each state. For example, Colorado A is the area in Montezuma County in and around Mesa Verde, and Colorado B includes La Plata County. The number following the B for La Plata County refers to particular sets of four townships, each on a topographic map. For instance, CO B:9:1 would refer to the first site in the four township set designated as 9 north of Durango.

Flora added to the complexity of the system in La Plata County by giving each township within the Gila Pueblo designation a separate number, which he would then assign to sites that he had personally recorded. So, a site designated by Flora as Colo B:21:XX would be designated as Colo B:13:XX by Gila Pueblo.

Added to this are sites that are designated Ignacio XX:XX. Ignacio was the name of the USGS map used by Flora and others in the 1930s to plot their sites in and around Durango. The numbers and letters after the Ignacio prefix refer both to individual segments of the quadrangle and to individual sites.

Unfortunately, the different designation systems have never been correlated in southwestern Colorado, although the Tree Ring Laboratory has done substantial work in trying to locate sites with Gila Pueblo and Flora site numbers in Colorado as part of their tree-ring studies.

SHERDS AND POINTS

The Archaeological Story of Durango, Colorado,
By Local Amateurs
(By Zeke)

Volume II   Number XII

Time: 620 A. D.

Place: Prehistoric ruin: "Ignacio 12:1" near Durango, Colo.

Narrator: The clan's chieftain.

Well, stranger, I haven't seen you all winter. Am glad you dropped by this fine spring day. Stick around if you can. All hands and the cook are joining in making up a batch of pottery and I know it will be a novel experience for you.

The youngsters returned the other evening with the report that the clay beds had thawed out so the

last few days the clan have been busily engaged in preparation for today's events.

A large quantity of clay was brought down to Junction creek and "refined". The refining process is done in a large hole in the ground that is lined in the bottom and on the sides with rock slabs. Into this cyst or vat is poured the raw clay and covered with water.

This mixture is stirred and stirred and more water added until it becomes the thickness, or rather the thinness, of the pancake batter you made last fall. After thoroughly stirring again, the material is allowed to stand until the water has all seeped off through the cracks and into the ground. The coarse material all goes to the bottom and the fine material comes to the top. The "potter" chooses the grade of

clay he or she wishes to use and the rest is discarded.

Clean sharp sand and finely crushed rock must be gotten for tempering material. If we attempted to bake the pure clay it would shrivel and crack even as it dried out. Here again the potters of the clan oversee the work.

The clay and tempering material are thoroughly mixed and allowed to stand for a period of time. This procedure would remind you of a stone mason as he prepared his mor-

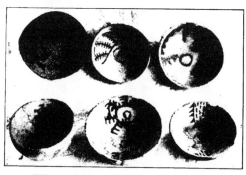

THESE HIEROGLYPHICS DEFY TRANSLATION

tar in advance. The moisture content is carefully watched so that the resulting paste will be as pliable as a child's modelling clay.

Materials for decorating the bowls must be obtained and used while still fresh. Our paint is simply the juice or sap of any and all vegetable matter. We use no extra pigments what-so-ever although I must admit that the mixture is usually very cloudy, to put it mildly.

Don't look at me in that tone of voice, stranger. I'm not stringing you. You see we put the paint on the damp "green" clay and the firing causes a chemical action that seals the carbon and other impurities against being released by the firing blaze. Our finished "paint" is in reality a fused layer of porcelain or crockery on the surface of

pottery. Moderns call it a glaze or vitreous paint. Sure. Why not?

If man of the 20th century wishes to "slag over" or vitrify a portion of exposed fire-brick in a kiln or furnace that is subjected to a great heat he simply uses salt. After our vegetable paint has been exposed to the heat for a little while, practically all that is left is the vegetable salts. That is the reason that our Basket Maker III paint will stand exposure to the sun and rain for 1,500 years and in some cases be brighter than when we made it. Compare our methods to scientific man's attempt to make paint. I believe we have the better technique.

Ordinarily we only paint on the inside of our bowls. I can't tell you why, I just don't know, but almost invariably we draw a circle in the center of the bowl. Around this we draw one, two, or more of our hieroglyphics to form a color contrast. The maker daubs the paint on the wet clay with a stick, using his or her own choice of symbol. Yes, each hieroglyphic or symbol has a meaning to us. It is our written alphabet of about 50 "letters".

You of course recognize our human figures, pictures of animals, sun symbols and a few others but I doubt if you can read our stories of hunting trips, deaths, fire, pestilence, the number in the clan, and many other records we left for you. Our "rosetta stone" was lost forever when our people joined forces with the X-culture of the south to make that great and powerful nation of pre-historic man known as the Pueblo Indians.

For a century after the merger there was an incessant struggle for supremacy between the makers of the two distinct kinds of pottery. In the end our Basket Maker product was entirely replaced by the superior pottery, more pleasing design, but inferior paint of the X-culture. Only in the Mimbres river valley was a compromise struck in which the design and the hieroglyphic were carried on together.

Well, I see the fires are all started in the firing rings. I'll can the chatter while we watch. Yes, those are the new vessels setting in the center with a four foot circle of open fire around them. They are getting black as the damp, raw clay absorbs smoke. Those bowls propped in place facing the fire are all decorated but you cannot see it now.

After the fire gets hotter and the smoke dies down you will get a les-

4.1 Front page of *Sherds and Points*. Notice the folksy writing style and the reference to the mysterious X-Culture. Courtesy, Center of Southwest Studies, Fort Lewis College.

used for these southwestern surveys was to collect a sample of pot-sherds from the surface of each site; this technique enabled them to compare ceramic types as one means of identifying the cultural differences of the southwestern peoples. Ironically, when Smith and Amundsen, forgot to follow this procedure in the Durango area, their forgetfulness laid the foundation for much of the future work that would be done in Durango, for the Gila Pueblo then had to contract with two local amateur archaeologists—Zeke Flora and the Reverend Homer Root—to collect the sherds that were missed by the survey team. In 1935, Flora and Root collected ceramics from the sites Smith and Amundsen had recorded, and they began visiting new sites and recording their locations on U.S. Geological Survey (USGS) maps. They also began an extensive program of excavation to recover wooden beams from prehistoric sites. The wood samples they collected would play a key role in the develop-ment of the tree-ring-dating method in southwestern archaeology.

These two men, along with Helen Sloan Daniels, were to lead archaeological work in the Durango area for the next two decades, even publishing a local archaeology magazine called *Sherds and Points* (Figure 4.1). Homer Root came into his own in Durango archaeology in the 1960s (we shall talk about him later in this book), but the 1930s were dominated by the two giants of Durango ar-chaeology, Helen Sloan Daniels and Zeke Flora, people of different background and education but united by their interest in the past. Many of the personal notes of these three pioneering amateur ar-cheologists were deposited in the archives of the Center of South-west Studies at Fort Lewis College.

At this point, we should mention that we had a very hard time deciding how to treat these three individuals. None of them had ever received any formal training in archaeology, and all of them, to varying degrees (Flora and Root in particular), engaged in what could only be called pothunting. The notes of their excavations also leave much to be desired—as did some of their interpreta-tions. Moreover, Flora's relationship with the professional archae-ologists of his day deteriorated to the point of mutual accusations and even lawsuits. As professionals ourselves, we cannot condone that type of behavior, and certainly it must never be repeated.

And yet we are left with a curious sympathy for these individu-

4.2 Helen Sloan Daniels. Courtesy, Center of Southwest Studies, Fort Lewis College.

als, even for Flora, who is often portrayed as the archvillain of Durango archaeology. These were not just run-of-the-mill pothunters. They did leave behind some record of their activities, frustrating though some of these may be, and in producing *Sherds and Points*, they at least made an effort to communicate their findings to the wider public. Perhaps it is best simply to say that they were products of their generation—an age when archaeology was not the sophisticated discipline it is today and a time in which some professional archaeologists themselves had started off as pothunters. We would never want such activities repeated today, of course, and we are well aware that many colleagues will disagree with our treatment of these individuals. But perhaps we should not rush to judge 1930s' behavior with 1990s' ethics.

Helen Sloan Daniels (1899–1979) was a member of one of the oldest families in the city (see Figure 4.2). She taught school for a little while and in 1921 married Dr. Frank C. Daniels, a local dentist. Her appetite for archaeology was first whetted by the ruins at

Mesa Verde National Park and the artifacts that city crews were accidentally unearthing at a gravel pit on Junction Street in Durango.

With the assistance of professional archaeologists such as Earl Morris, Daniels undertook her own excavations at various sites in and around Durango between 1936 and 1940. Her excavations were sponsored by the National Youth Administration, a federal program that provided various types of employment for youths during the Great Depression. Her objectives were numerous. First, she wished to gather a comprehensive display of artifacts for a proposed museum in the public library. Second, she wanted to uncover pithouses to document their architectural development. Third, she hoped to recover as many tree-ring specimens as possible to assist in building an absolute chronology for the area. Fourth, she wanted to concentrate on sites that were in danger of being destroyed by city and highway construction projects, a prospect that truly alarmed her.

Daniels's excavations were mainly limited to large Basketmaker III sites located within the city limits. The results of her work were published in 1940 in *Sherds and Points* and in a monograph entitled *The Durango Public Library Project*. Much of this second document was devoted to administrative detail and the problems of supervising her "boys," who, in fact, ranged in age from 16 to 25 and who were paid $.37 per hour for a maximum of 44 hours per month.

Daniels's own objectives, together with the general tone of archaeology at that time, produced manuscripts that, to contemporary archaeologists, might appear highly selective in their recording and interpretation of data; for instance, her descriptions of sites, their locations, and their artifacts are often frustratingly vague. However, it is easy to criticize with the luxury of hindsight. Daniels's work is to be commended, for it helped cement Durango's importance in Southwest archaeology. Moreover, we defy anyone who reads her book not to come away with a sense of her total commitment to and love for the past of her town. In her writings, there is a humility toward her subject that is touching and heartwarming.

The other giant of Durango archaeology was Isaiah Ford "Zeke" Flora (Figure 4.3), the son of an Ohio minister. Born in 1901, Flora moved to Durango in 1933, and his life seems to have been consumed by attempts to find the job that would make him a rich man.

4.3 I. F. "Zeke" Flora. Courtesy, Center of Southwest Studies, Fort Lewis College.

He tried his hand, for example, at uranium prospecting and scientific technical writing, all the while running a local jewelry shop. He died in 1979.

Soon after his arrival in Durango, Flora developed an intense interest in the archaeology of the area. Harold Gladwin and A. E. Douglass taught him the rudiments of dendrochronology and asked him to collect as many samples as possible for study at the Gila Pueblo Laboratory in Arizona. Flora surveyed large portions of the Upper Animas valley, located the famous Basketmaker II sites in Falls Creek, and trenched a vast number of sites for tree-ring specimens. Unfortunately, like Daniels, he did not precisely locate some of these sites in his written records, and his work as a whole was not always well documented. Yet this work holds a special position in Southwest archaeology, for it contributed substantially to the con-

HOBBIES	PROFESSIONS
GRAVE ROBBER	DENDROCHRONOLOGIST
GAME EXTERMINATOR	ARCHAEOLOGIST
MUMMY EXCAVATOR	HOROLOGIST

I. F. (ZEKE) FLORA

1617 W. 2nd Ave.

DURANGO, COLO.

Merchant's Wholesale Watch Repairing

OUTSTANDING FAILURES	SPECIALTIES
MOVIE ACTOR	MAKING A-BOMBS
AUTHOR & WRITER	COUNTERFEITING
LABORER	DERMOGATING

4.4 Flora's business card. Courtesy, Center of Southwest Studies, Fort Lewis College.

struction of an absolute chronology for the area. His work in dendrochronology was officially recognized in 1939 when he was elected a fellow of the Tree-Ring Society.

As Flora continued working at sites in Durango, he honed his skills as a field archaeologist, but it is still difficult to locate exactly many of the sites he excavated. Some notes were made and some photos taken, and these survive today in the records at the University of Arizona, but they were haphazardly done and are difficult to relate to specific sites. There is no question that Flora tried to adopt the methods of the archaeologists he had worked with, but the results were erratic at best.

Flora also tried his hand at interpretation. For example, he believed there had been a major cultural and physical split between Basketmaker III and Pueblo I peoples, and he postulated that an unknown group of people—the "X-Culture—had merged with the Basketmakers to create the Pueblo I peoples. Modern archaeologists, of course, seem more comfortable with the idea that there was instead an internal development of Pueblo I from Basketmaker III.

Flora was often at the center of controversy. Because of his lack of training and his propensity to excavate with little forethought, making few notes along the way, he was regarded by many archaeologists as no better than a pothunter; the *Durango Herald News* of February 13, 1955, for example, referred to him as "the bad boy of American Archaeology." Indeed, Zeke himself must have recognized the duality of his character, as reflected in the business card that he carried and gave away freely (shown in Figure 4.4).

The lengthy correspondence between Flora and archaeologists at the University of Arizona and Gila Pueblo makes it very clear that everything he excavated, including the prehistoric wood samples, was for sale. In fact, particularly in the early days of his career in Durango, he was often paid for the objects he collected. Generally, these artifacts were purchased by Harold Gladwin, a practice that Gladwin carried out throughout the Southwest. In those day, this was not the radical sin it would be today (although it does raise the hoary ethical dilemma that archaeologists have always faced about whether it is better to reward pothunters by purchasing their wares and thus preserving the objects in public institutions or to reject the items as having been illicitly and unscientifically collected). In any case, Flora went too far when he tried to sell the Falls Creek material, material that had been removed from public lands. He contacted the American Civil Liberties Union (ACLU) as late as 1968 to get help in securing money that he believed was owed to him by Mesa Verde National Park; the ACLU turned him down.

The professional archaeological community's tolerance for Flora and his work finally ran out in 1941, after a reporter from *Life* magazine met Flora in Durango and proposed a full-page article about his colorful career. An archaeologist at Mesa Verde National Park, Don Watson, heard about the proposed story and wrote to several of his colleagues, saying that the professional community should not encourage such publicity. A number of nationally known archaeologists—including Jesse Nusbaum, the Department of Interior consulting archaeologist, and numerous archaeologists from Arizona to Harvard—expressed their concerns to Henry Luce, the publisher of the magazine, and urged him not to publish the article. The article was never written.

This event effectively terminated the relationship between Flora and the professional archaeological community. However, Zeke maintained his relationship with the Laboratory of Tree-Ring Re-

4.5 Homer Root.

search for many years. Indeed, the laboratory still houses the Flora Collection of tree-ring specimens, one of the most important collections for dating the early part of Anasazi prehistory. For many years, Flora also continued to correspond with Jeffrey Dean, the current head of the laboratory's archaeological-dating section.

How, then, should we evaluate Flora's position in Durango and southwestern archaeology? We cannot deny that his work in tree-ring dating and excavating sites in the Durango area was nothing short of phenomenal. But what should we make of those activities that turned the professional community away from him? Perhaps those of us who enjoy the comforts of middle-class, professional life today should attempt to view Flora's activities in context. We should remember that he was trying to make ends meet during the Great Depression while working with moneyed middle- and upper-class Americans (Gladwin, for example, was a millionaire). It may be entirely understandable that such a man would try to maximize his profits under those conditions, and we, living our comfortable, middle-class, professional lives, should not rush to judgment.

And what of Flora's propensity to excavate and not record his findings? In truth, that failing is not unique to Flora or to amateur

BOX 4.2
THE ROOT PORTFOLIOS

One of the greatest testimonies to the devotion of amateur archaeologists in the American Southwest is the series of portfolios in old-fashioned legal ledgers that Homer Root produced, which are on file in the Center of Southwest Studies at Fort Lewis College. As curator of the college's museum, Root was responsible for creating an inventory of all the materials that the museum possessed and for documenting the results of his field schools in Ridges Basin. What Root produced were not the run-of-the-mill, sterile museum inventory and site reports; rather, they were a set of writings that not only fulfill their museum inventory function but also give more than a glimpse into the mind of a gifted and devoted antiquarian (Figures 4.6, 4.7, and 4.8).

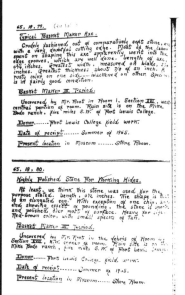

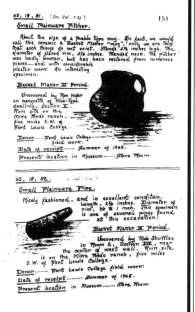

4.6 Example of Root's artifact inventory. The original figures are painted in color. The two pages are from the inventory of his 1965 excavation in Ridges Basin. Courtesy, Center of Southwest Studies, Fort Lewis College.

RESUME OF FIELD NOTES.   27

IX.: EXCAVATION OF THE SECOND BUILDING PROJECT ON THE RIDGE.
A. THE SECOND PIT-HOUSE.

Following the fire which destroyed most of the structures on our "sacred ridge," a new but less extensive building program was initiated. How much time elapsed between the conflagration and the second effort is questionable..... we lack datings as yet..... but our impression is that the new building project started soon after the fire. Admittedly, our conviction is influenced by the feeling that the ridge played a significant role in the life of all the area inhabitants.

At this point in our report, a very unusual factor enters the narration. Obviously, in the natural development of the second building project, and in the progress of our excavations, this is the place to write about the second pit-house, and we shall do what is expected. However, the second pit-house actually was the last structure we excavated on the ridge. For better than three months we did not know that such a part of the ruin existed. Reason? Hard, yellow clay from the third pit-house had been dumped into the second pit-house centuries past, with the result that hundreds of years of weathering caused it to appear as undisturbed soil. In truth, our discovery of this structure was almost accidental.

One of our young men had started a prospect hole in the fill near rooms we were excavating. It seemed a waste of time, because the clay did appear as virgin soil. But a few bits of discoloration made us wonder, so the young man continued enlarging the hole and digging deeper. Finally, at a depth of about 5½ feet, he broke through the clay into a thick deposit of burned material. By this time, the digger was in serious difficulty, for his "pit" was only some thirty inches long and eighteen inches wide. After resorting to the tricks of a contortionist, he was able to clean out the hole, striking a plastered floor at seven feet. He then came up with the statement that his "pit" was plastered on all four sides! The claim was unbelievable, but we were very busy with other discoveries at the moment, and so let it stand.

Our excavations grew more exciting and demanding by the day, and thus we deliberately ignored further investigation of the deep hole for quite a period. However, on each occasion when I passed that way my irritation increased. In the first place, no digger could possibly have such luck as to go right down on a "plastered pit" exactly fitting the dimensions of his experimental excavation. In the second place, such a pit could have no excuse for existing in that location.

Others in the party began to have similar doubts concerning the "plastered hole." Then, one of the young ladies volunteered to do some additional exploring in the pit. Within a very short time she confirmed the plastered floor and

4.7 Example of Root's writings. This section describes how one of the pithouses was excavated in 1966. Courtesy, Center of Southwest Studies, Fort Lewis College.

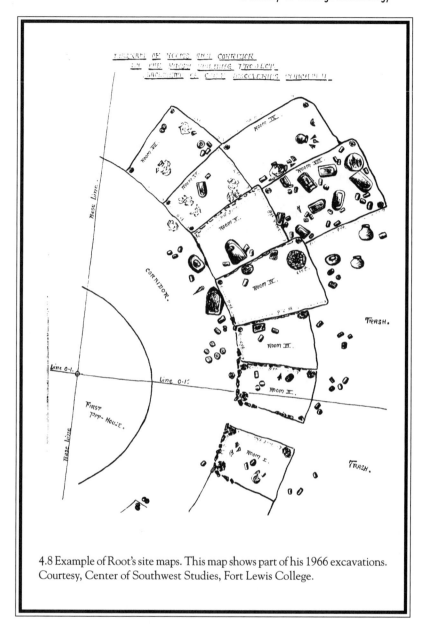

4.8 Example of Root's site maps. This map shows part of his 1966 excavations. Courtesy, Center of Southwest Studies, Fort Lewis College.

archaeologists in general. And while there is at least one professional archaeologist who has excavated a site and not published the results in a timely manner, then condemnations of Flora by professionals have more than a hint of hypocrisy.

In any case, World War II brought an end to this early phase of Durango archaeology. Flora, for instance, went off to war work. The 1940s and 1950s were relatively quiet. Archaeological sites continued to be unearthed as the town grew and new buildings sprouted up, but the almost frantic activity of the 1930s was not repeated.

It was not until the 1960s that new investigations started, and these were in the hands of Homer Root (Figure 4.5). Root (1896–1977) became the pastor of the First Methodist Church in Durango in 1930. He began doing archaeological work with Daniels and Flora in the 1930s, and on his retirement from the ministry in 1953, he formed a liaison with Fort Lewis College, serving as the school's museum curator and, from 1965 to 1969, running its field schools in Ridge Basin.

Root's work concentrated on large pithouse structures that would yield a good artifact collection and information on pithouse architecture (remember that he was a child of the 1930s, so these goals were very important to him). He left behind a series of portfolios documenting all his work in Ridges Basin, as well as a number of exhibits featuring points and other artifacts affixed to boards. Unfortunately, among his other technical failings, he did not collect everything that he excavated—a must even then—and so much valuable information was lost. And as his writings make clear, he had a chip on his shoulder about professional archaeologists. As with the other amateur archaeologists of Durango, we can perhaps applaud his attentions, but we must decry his techniques (see Box 4.2)

Beyond the intrinsic contribution he made to Durango archaeology through his work in the basin, Root also showed administrators at Fort Lewis College the attractiveness of formalizing the teaching of archaeology, and in 1966, they hired a professional archaeologist, John C. Ives, a Ph.D. from Harvard University. Ives worked for two seasons in Ridges Basin. Interestingly, his own field school coincided with some of Root's, which were also held in the basin, and there was a degree of animosity between the amateur and the professional. Ives used to tell the hilarious story about the two crews working virtually within shouting distance of each other but never even visiting one another's sites.

Ives established the first formal anthropology program at Fort Lewis College. His knowledge of the basic data of the Southwest was nothing short of phenomenal, and he taught generations of students the basics of Southwestern prehistory. Unfortunately, Ives never produced formal site reports on any of his excavations for the college. (Sadly, he passed away in 1996 after only a few years of retirement.)

Ives also laid the foundations for the close undergraduate-faculty collaboration in research that has since been the cornerstone of the department's teaching philosophy. This philosophy has been followed by the three archaeologists who now teach in the department: Susan Riches, hired in 1971; Philip Duke, hired in 1980; and Jim Judge, hired in 1990. In 1993, Mona Charles was appointed a research associate in the department.

Another prominent local contribution to Durango and southwestern scholarship was the founding of Fort Lewis College's Center of Southwest Studies in 1964. This unique research and teaching institute was made possible by a gift from the Ballantine family of Durango, which has always supported the college and the study of Southwest cultures. The center's first director was the historian Robert Delaney, a scholar of Ute history, and under him, the college's commitment to southwestern scholarship grew and prospered.

The development of archaeological conservation laws in the 1970s had a great impact on Durango archaeology. This is best exemplified in the work conducted in Ridges Basin by (employees of) the environmental and archaeological consulting firm ESCA-TECH. The survey they produced alleviated some of the deficiencies in our understanding of Durango's past. For one thing, it constituted the first large-scale archaeological investigation in the Durango area. For another, it expanded the database beyond the Basketmaker pithouses that had traditionally been the focus of attention to encompass pre-Anasazi sites as well as the remains of the later Ute, Navajo, and Euroamericans.

The work of Francis Smiley and his students in Ridges Basin, John Gooding's work in the Bodo Industrial Park, Steven Fuller's in Bodo Canyon, and, most recently, Mona Charles's work, also in the Bodo Industrial Park as well as north of Durango, have been made possible only by the federal and state laws that protect archaeological sites. Charles's important work is particularly significant in that her funding has come from private citizens who own land but who have gone beyond legal requirements to enable her to fully document the archaeological sites damaged during construction.

The federal government has played a substantial role in the development of archaeological research in Durango and the Four Corners area ever since the creation of Mesa Verde National Park. The federal government supported the work of Helen Sloan Daniels in 1930s with funding through the Works Project Administration. Durango also houses the offices of archaeologists working for the U.S. Forest Service, the Bureau of Reclamation, and the Bureau of Land Management. Today, these agencies, in partnership with Fort Lewis College and local archaeological groups, continue to survey nearby federal land for archaeological and historical sites.

A good example of this partnership is found at Falls Creek. In 1993, the Forest Service, with the assistance of the Trust of Public Land and the La Plata Open Space Council, acquired some 500 acres of land within the Falls Creek valley. To this, the Forest Service added nearby lands and established the Falls Creek Archaeological Area to recognize and preserve this important archaeological locale for the American public. A trail to the South Shelter was constructed in 1994, but the site has since been closed to the public to protect it and in deference to the wishes of Native American tribes who view the site as sacred. Unfortunately, the site continues to be subject to vandalism.

Also important in local historical education is the Animas Museum, run by Robert McDaniel and Charles Ferdinando. This little gem of a museum at the north end of town provides an intimate setting for the teaching of Durango's past. It offers regular programs for local schoolchildren and sponsors a summer lecture series on Durango's past that is well attended by residents and tourists alike. Recently, the Children's Museum of Durango was opened in the Durango Arts Center as another means of involving the city's children in the study of the past. A newly completed river trail system incorporates informational plaques pointing out the history and archaeology of the Animas valley.

We cannot leave the history of Durango archaeology without returning to the base of our knowledge of Durango's past—the dedicated amateur community. The San Juan chapter of the Colorado Archaeological Society, a statewide group of avocational and amateur archaeologists interested in learning about and protecting Colorado's past, was established in 1979 by Helen Sloan Daniels and Charles Brockway. The influence of these prominent individuals on the course of the new chapter was brief, however, for Daniels died that same year, and Brockway went on to a career in the navy.

Their mantle was taken over by John Sanders, a geologist who had lived on Durango's Crestview Drive in the 1950s (very close to Helen Sloan Daniels's site in Delwood Circle, in fact). He retired back to Durango in 1978 and has been a guiding force in the San Juan chapter ever since. John is one of two original charter members who are still active in the chapter. The other is Jill Tripp, who received her B.A. in Spanish and anthropology from the University of Colorado in 1973.

The San Juan chapter's membership (over 230 in 1997) is the largest among all the chapters in the state. The chapter has a very full field program, with a special emphasis on visiting the numerous rock-art sites of the Four Corners area. Many of their members have completed the Program for Avocational Archaeological Certification (PAAC) so that they can assist professional archaeologists in basic site survey, excavation, and analysis. For example, Cheryle Braandsma, a local resident, was an invaluable participant in the Red Lion excavations and also worked on the Tamarron Cabin project. Chapter members regularly help federal archaeologists in survey and excavation work, and they have often worked with Fort Lewis College archaeologists on excavations in the San Juan National Forest since 1991. Just as important, the chapter, along with its parent organization, continues to lobby government for continued vigilance in the protection and conservation of archaeological sites.

This public commitment to archaeology has made Durango the only city in the state and one of the few in the country to have an ordinance specifically designed to protect archaeological sites (this will be discussed in more detail in Chapter 5). It is entirely appropriate that a town with such a historical commitment to archaeology should hold this honor.

Clearly, public participation in the study of Durango's past is alive and well. And despite the constant threats to the historical fabric of the community, we feel confident that its residents will continue to exercise vigilance in protecting the past.

5

Protecting the Past: Durango's Example

Americans are world leaders in terms of the attention they devote to their archaeological past. They spend millions of dollars, in both public and private funds, in locating and preserving historic and prehistoric remains. Unfortunately, however, unlike most other countries concerned with guarding the past, the United States by and large has legislated protection only in regard to federal lands. The two-thirds of American territory that lies in private hands has no protection, and the loss of prehistoric and historic resources is staggering.

Most other countries have laws that protect historic and archaeological remains on both public *and* private lands. These countries apply to the protection of the past the same logic that is applied to protecting wildlife, water, and air (the concept being that people don't own the water that flows through their property or the air they breathe). Although it would probably be a mistake to try to force such legislation on a country that is almost obsessive about protecting private ownership rights, the case for doing so should certainly be put forward to all of the American public as another means of safeguarding the past. Perhaps an honorable compromise would be to work to convince landowners of the importance of archaeological sites on their property and to help them preserve these sites with such inducements as tax credits. But for now, local communities can do a great deal to preserve their archaeological resources.

Durango is essentially no different from most other towns and cities in America, in that beneath its streets and lawns lie the remains of the past. What makes Durango different is that its citizens have acted to protect some of this past. The town is a leader among communities in the American West in its attempt to preserve both its European and its Native American remains. In 1983, the city of Durango contracted with us to prepare a city ordinance designed to protect archaeological sites in the city from damage or destruction by construction projects, both public and private. The initiative for getting the policy enacted was taken by two men who were on the city council at the time: Ian "Sandy" Thompson, affiliated with the Crow Canyon Center for American Archaeology located near Cortez and a leader in developing public archaeology programs for many years (sadly, he passed away a few years ago), and Ira Plotkin, once a faculty member at Fort Lewis College and now a dean at Teikyo–Loretto Heights College in Denver.

For a time, Durango actually had a city archaeologist who was paid to exercise the ordinance regulations and to work with developers to ensure that valuable sites were not destroyed whenever possible. Although that position is now inactive, Jill Seyfarth of the City Planner's Office still sees that development is monitored.

The community has placed its historic downtown on the National Register of Historic Places, and it maintains an active Historic Preservation Board to encourage businesses and private homeowners to maintain and preserve their historic buildings and houses. The Third Avenue Boulevard, one of the older and nicer neighborhoods in town, has been added to the National Register and most recently to the city's own local register of historic places, so that the avenue's historic character and charm will be preserved for future generations. In addition, owners of numerous historic structures throughout the city have received grants from the State Historical Society to maintain and restore their properties.

The *Durango Herald*, under the direction of the Ballantine family, continues its longtime support of archaeological and historic preservation by publishing articles about the history and archaeology of Durango on the first Tuesday of every month. These articles, written by members of the Historic Preservation Board, keep the issue of preserving the past in the public eye.

6
The End of Our Story— and the Beginning

At the outset of this book, we stated that all of us, but especially archaeologists and historians, help to create the past by the questions we ask and the assumptions we make. We want to close the book by saying a little more on why we believe archaeology is more than an intellectual entertainment, as well as offering some insights on how all of us can use the past to understand and serve the present. We don't pose any specific questions, and, certainly, we offer no answers—it is our goal, instead, to simply present some examples of archaeology's potential.

Let's look first at how archaeologists have viewed the environment and its relationship to past peoples, their population sizes, and their ways of life. Archaeology has a special place in this endeavor because of all the Western sciences, it alone offers us such a long-term perspective on the nature of the relationship between humans and the natural environment.

Durango's archaeology gives us warning signs about the dangers of overpopulating an area like the Animas valley. In Chapter 4, we described how the seventh and eighth centuries saw a massive population movement into the valley, caused by worsening drought conditions elsewhere and, for a while at least, an improving environment in the Upper Animas valley. At the end of the eighth century, however, drought conditions caught up with Durango, and the result was the apparent collapse of the Basketmaker-Pueblo occupation of the valley.

Such an event has more than academic archaeological interest, for similar conditions are currently being experienced in the Durango area. Even as the population increases because of the area's attractiveness, there is mounting uncertainty about the availability of key resources. To this point, all we archaeologists have done is wag our fingers and say we know what might happen. But archaeologists must do more—they must actually get this information into the public arena, so that people become aware of the potential consequences.

Such concerns can be taken further, even into the realm of politics. Our way has been shown by those archaeologists who are analyzing how archaeology has inadvertently conditioned society's views of females. For example, even a simple and apparently harmless thing such as using the term *mankind* instead of *humankind* can inadvertently devalue females and minimize their importance in both present and past society. Assuming that females have always made the pots and males have always hunted (without actually demonstrating this with archaeological data) also can serve to stereotype female behavior in our own society. It is telling that although no specific studies of this type have been conducted in Durango archaeology, all of us working in the area have implicitly assumed this particular sexual division of labor. So, one lesson we can draw from the feminist critique of archaeology is to be careful about the messages we send regarding human relations.

The Pueblo people apply a number of different terms to the prehistoric groups that archaeologists generally lump together under the term *Anasazi*. Their terms are specific to each group's language and their own past. They also consider different things in their past to be important. The Hopi, for example, place great importance on the migration routes and early homes of their different clan groups. Where did a clan come from? What were its travels before it came to Hopi? What events took place along the way? The Hopi view this migration as an important part of their history, something that generally occurs without reference to time, which, as noted, is a concept of great importance to Anglo-American archaeologists.

Even the term *Anasazi* is now under fire, and we suspect that the word will by and large cease to be used early in the twenty-first century. Modern Pueblo Indians, whose ancestors are most certainly the

Anasazi, do not want archaeologists to use the term at all anymore. The term is, in fact, a Navajo word that has been variously translated as "Ancient Ones" or "Enemy Ancestors." A word that seems a good replacement for *Anasazi* is *Ancestral Pueblo*. However, we should point out that not even renaming the Anasazi is a settled matter, for many Navajo believe that their own ancestors may have been responsible for some Anasazi sites. This problem will take many years to sort out, and it is but one example of how modern-day politics increasingly intrude into archaeological interpretation.

This very book provides a good example of the way in which inadvertent messages can be communicated, for by organizing the data chronologically, from Paleoindian to Historic, we have concentrated on technological change as a means of breaking the past into manageable units. One message we may be sending, therefore, is that contemporary Western society, with its emphasis on technological innovation, is the climax of this evolution.

However, nothing compels us to organize the past in that way. Many Native American societies, for instance, do not have a conception of *linear* time, and they do not see the need to chop up the past the way we do. Larry Zimmerman, an archaeologist, has devoted many years to bringing Native Americans and archaeologists together. Relying on the work of the Native American scholar and activist Vine Deloria Jr. and others, Zimmerman has argued that many Native Americans see the past as part of the present; that is, the past is never *past*. Thus, when archaeologists talk about the past as a period that is *gone* or *over*, they do a profound injustice to those Native Americans because they imply that their present is extinct as well.

Another example of how modern European-American values have influenced our study of the past involves the way in which archaeologists have placed little relative emphasis on the study of the Ute as compared to the Ancestral Pueblo. Few archaeologists would disagree with the statement that when it comes to the study of the Southwest, the Ute have gotten short shrift from most archaeologists in the field. The Ute did not build spectacular pueblos like those in New Mexico and Arizona, nor did they have a tradition of making beautiful pottery. And so, beginning with the earliest explorers and antiquarians, this tribe has been overlooked. That oversight is partly seen in this book's description of Durango archaeology, for we have concentrated on the pithouse cultures because they were most easily found in the recent past and because their sites are more visually attractive than another culture's scatter of lithic flakes or overnight hunting camps.

However, we can look at this issue from another angle, one that makes the Ute much more significant in terms of understanding the best way to live in this part of the world. Anthropologists estimate that 99 percent of all human existence has been devoted to the hunter-gatherer lifestyle. Consequently, if we had to choose a lifestyle that we knew worked well for humans, it would have to be hunting and gathering. Put in that light, the chronology of Durango archaeology can be viewed differently; we can see that in the Durango area, human occupation for the last 10,000 years has been primarily oriented to hunting and gathering, while attempts at farming and a sedentary lifestyle, by contrast, have been short-lived (and in the Basketmaker-Pueblo case, "unsuccessful" over the long haul). What does this mean for our own society?

Although these arguments might seem a little far-fetched, we are not alone in making them. Archaeologists all over the world, of different ethnic, gender, and class backgrounds, are beginning to see the extraordinary opportunity archaeology has to offer a vibrant and relevant commentary on modern society. We can use the past to define different ways by which society can be organized, and we can demonstrate that the social structures of Western society are not the only patterns in which humans can exist.

Native Americans across the continent have always realized how important the past is. They talk about who "owns" the past, and they are making strenuous efforts to regain a voice in how their past is portrayed. Some archaeologists have resisted this approach on the grounds that it weakens the scientific value of their field. We are not members of that camp: instead, we argue that we need to break down the walls of mistrust between archaeologists and Native Americans and get both sides working together.

For many years, archaeologists, almost all of whom are from white American society, conducted the primary research not only on the Anasazi but also on much Native American history and prehistory in general. And for the most part, Native American oral traditions were ignored or even refuted by the archaeologists. Many Native Americans resent the intrusion of white scholars and scientists into something as important and personal as their past.

Since the late 1980s or so, Native Americans have been taking more control of their own past (just as they are doing with the economies, politics, and other aspects of life), and they now insist on having a much stronger voice in the dialogue on how their past is interpreted and taught. For example, the archaeologists' great interest in fragments of pottery, the size and shape of kivas, and other such information often is of little concern to them. This transformation toward including Native American people and their viewpoints and beliefs has been painful for many archaeologists.

Perhaps the best example of how Native Americans have become actively involved in archaeology is the passing in 1990 of the Native American Graves Protection and Repatriation Act. This federal law requires all museums and universities that hold Native American human remains, as well as objects such as grave goods, to turn these over to the tribe that claims descent from the remains. These skeletal remains and grave goods can then be reburied with the appropriate religious ceremonies.

Both of us are of European descent, and we've both been trained in a particular way, so it is hard to change our own way of thinking. That does not mean, though, that somebody else cannot break out of that traditional mold and devise a new way of looking at the past. After all, archaeology has only been around for a couple of hundred years, and our way of studying the past is certainly not carved in stone. Ultimately, re-creating the past should not mean choosing between different versions, such as the archaeological version and the Native American version. Rather, we should acknowledge that all versions have legitimate elements, and archaeologists should try to form an alliance with others so that these different versions of the past can be at least partially reconciled.

CONCLUSION

We hope that in reading this book, you've captured some of the flavor not just of Durango archaeology but also of archaeology in general. For both of us, learning about the archaeological past of our town has been one of the great pleasures of our lives. We have worked as professional archaeologists in many parts of the world, but in very few places have we ever felt so connected to the archaeological past—it's all around us as we drive to the supermarket or take our children to school—and to those amateurs and professionals who came here full of hope and enthusiasm, determined to put Durango on the archaeological map.

We also hope that you have a better idea of where Durango fits into the wider picture of archaeology. As we've seen, Durango occupies a pivotal place in the development of southwestern archaeology, and study of the area is still affected by wider social and intellectual currents.

Finally, we hope that you see why the study of the past is so important to us in the present. Please join with us in our efforts to preserve as much of that past as we can. We cannot save every site, but we can try to ensure that as little knowledge as possible is lost. And above all, we urge you to regard the past as something that *you* can have a hand in creating. It is too important to be left to the professionals alone.

Appendix
The Major Archaeological Sites of Durango

In producing this more detailed appendix of archaeological sites, we have concentrated on remains from the Ancestral Pueblo period simply because this period has been more intensively studied than others. Additional Durango area sites are described in Chapter 3.

Falls Creek and the North End of Town

The excavations by Flora and Morris in the Falls Creek Rock Shelters produced a total of 44 human remains, the oldest tree-ring dates for any Anasazi site in the Southwest, the first substantiated house remains from the Basketmaker II period, and well-preserved basketry and sandals, stone tools, and other artifacts.

The South Shelter, the larger and more imposing of the 2 shelters in this area, produced surprisingly few archaeological remains. During his excavations, Morris found fragments of only 2 house structures and very few artifacts. It was apparent that although the South Shelter was used by the Basketmaker II peoples, they much preferred the North Shelter as a place for habitation.

The natural floor of the North Shelter slopes from north to south to form a series of 3 "terraces." These terraces were enlarged and flattened by the Basketmaker people, and structures were found on all 3. In all, Morris found 9 remains of floors of pit structures and associated features. These floors (most of the superstructures for the pithouses had long since deteriorated) were often superimposed on one another, indicating periods of occupation, reoccupation, and rebuilding.

The floors of the pit structures usually contained a central firepit, a prepared floor (that is, a floor covered with a coating of clay), and storage pits dug into the floor. Some of these were clay-lined basins; others were lined with rock.

Artifacts recovered during the excavations included a large variety of stone tools, stone pipes, bone awls, other tools of bone, sandals, baskets, cordage, aprons, bags, and other objects. The excavations produced personal items such as beads, necklaces, and other jewelry. In all, several thousand artifacts and fragments of corn, seeds, squashes, and other food items were found.

In addition to the structures and material culture in the rock shelters, the walls of both shelters contain a variety of prehistoric rock art attributable to either the Basketmaker II or Basketmaker III period. Human figures painted in green, black, and red clay are found in the North Shelter, and a variety of sticklike figures exist in the South Shelter. These panels are the best-known prehistoric rock art in the Durango area. Since the excavations and research were done at the Falls Creek area, archaeologist Jack Pfertsh has recorded a number of additional panels nearby. Archaeologists Sally Cole and Shirley Powell are currently undertaking a detailed study of the rock art, and their results are awaited with much anticipation.

Like the structures found at the rock shelters, Talus Village was composed of a series of floors built over one another, as though the residents had frequently remodeled them or replaced the floors as they became worn or dirty. Firepits and rock-lined storage pits similar to those in the caves were also very common.

One of the structures provided information on how the walls and roofing were probably constructed. Instead of the central vertical-beam roof supports that Morris had anticipated and that were commonly used in the following Basketmaker III period, the walls were constructed of relatively short beams laid horizontally on the ground and cross-hatched as the walls rose. The exterior of these walls was covered with adobe mud to provide waterproofing.

Talus Village also produced a large number of burials, some 34 in all. Many of the burials at Talus Village were found within the rock-lined storage pits in the structures, confirming that the Anasazi practice of burial close to or within their villages began long ago.

Roy Carlson's synthesis of Morris's excavations of the 6 Basketmaker

III pithouses helped to define a pattern typical for Durango and other parts of southwestern Colorado for the period between A.D. 700 and A.D. 800. The Anasazi of this time were living in fairly deep pithouses with connecting tunnels and antechambers. The typical pithouse was roofed by placing 4 to 6 vertical posts in the floor and building super-structures around the main support posts. The resulting structure was partially above ground and accessed by means of a ladder near the center of the roof. Outside, on the ground surface, a series of rooms, probably built for storage, formed a partial arc around the pithouse. These surface rooms were constructed of an adobe pole and mud frame-work. The resulting structure probably supported 1 or 2 families, with associated storage and work areas. Often, a ring of large rocks sur-rounded the pithouse and storage rooms. Artifacts associated with these Basketmaker III pithouses included many that had been found in the preceding period, but a number of new ones were introduced as well. Primary among these was a relatively simple type of gray pottery. Frag-ments of beans, added to the previous planted crops of corn and squash, indicate the people placed a growing reliance on farming.

Site 5LP 4991, the Darkmold Site, is 4.5 miles north of the Durango city limits on private property. The site was identified during foundation construction for the property owner's house. The following information was kindly provided by Mona Charles, cur-rently directing the Fort Lewis College field school at the site. We also acknowledge the great help provided by the landowner, Mark Dold, in facilitating the work

As of 1998, construction excavation in the western portion of the house site revealed three subsurface pit features. One of these, Struc-ture 1, most definitely represents a large pithouse with three primary occupational levels and several episodes of remodeling. A plain grayware sherd, found at the contact of one of two major occupations, places this occupation within the Basketmaker III period. Three samples for dendrochronological dating were extracted from the overlying fill of this structure. Another probable structure, Structure 2, is present north of Structure 1. This feature possessed several episodes of fill. A trash layer was deposited immediately above the floor, and several slope wash layers comprise the remaining structural fill. A single grayware sherd was removed from the upper fill of the structure; however, no dendrochronological samples were obtained from this feature. A third occupation was exposed in the profile below the southern portion of Structure 1. In profile, this occupation is denoted by a layer of charcoal and gray sediments that are truncated by Structure 1. A thick layer of fill with charcoal but no artifacts separates the uppermost fill of Structure 1 from the charcoal and gray sediments of the lower (earlier) occupation. A sample for radiocarbon dating was extracted from this layer. Among the macrobotanical specimens in the sample were burned corn kernels. This sample was radiocarbon-dated to 2170 B.P. ± 80 B.P. To date, thirteen burials have been recovered.

RIDGES BASIN

Site 5LP 171 was excavated by Homer Root in 1965. This site comprises a pithouse approximately 8 meters wide and 2 meters deep. The walls of the structure contained an earthen bench about 1 meter high, and on this bench were the remains of 8 postholes for the roof supports. Root did not describe any floor hearth, although he noted 2 "sand-pits" that may have served as heating pits. Twelve surface rooms formed an arc around the northwest part of the pithouse. These were defined by *jacal* ("burnt adobe") and upright sandstone slabs, which were probably wall footers.

Root recovered a variety of decorated grayware vessels, ceramic pipes, and grinding stones. A tree-ring date of A.D. 707–749 was taken from one of the beams in the pithouse. Architecturally, the site falls comfortably in the A.D. 650–800 period.

In 1966, Root and an 18-student crew returned for their most extensive and spectacular work in Ridges Basin. On a spur at the south end of the basin, Root excavated what he termed "Sacred Ridge," comprising 3 pithouses, 28 surface rooms, and at least 45 "human burials" (although not all of these burials actually had human remains). Because of the cluster of structures, as well as the wide range of pottery and stone material left behind, Root believed this ridge had been some sort of prehistoric trade center. This complex is now designated 5LP 245 (Figure A.1). The importance of this site in the overall political and social system of Ridges Basin is currently being investigated by Francis Smiley and his colleagues.

The first pithouse was approximately 7 meters in diameter and 2 meters deep. Two sand pits and 4 postholes were found in its floor.

A.1 Aerial view of Root's 1966 excavations. Note the arc of roomblocks surrounding the central pithouse.

Root uncovered a series of postholes outside the pithouse that appeared to lead to it; he interpreted this area as a covered walkway. As with 5LP 171, an arc of roomblocks was found on the west side of the structure. In 1 room, a slab-lined cist was found; another room yielded 8 metates and 15 manos, leading Root to speculate that this room was a specialized milling area. Tree-ring dates of A.D. 654 and 660 were taken from the pithouse and the roomblock.

The second pithouse was 4 meters in diameter and almost 2 meters deep. Like the others in the basin, it contained sand pits. This pithouse was flanked on its west by a row of 7 rooms. A tree-ring date of A.D. 651 was taken from a beam in the pithouse.

The third and largest pithouse was approximately 10 meters in diameter and almost 3 meters deep. It had 4 slab-lined postholes, 2 sand pits, and what Root described as a passageway into the southeast wall. It was in association with a row of 6 rooms. Two tree-ring dates of A.D. 608 and 667 were taken from wood fragments in the pithouse.

The other main feature of Sacred Ridge was what Root called a "dance-floor." Southwest of the first pithouse complex, he excavated a cleared earthen surface of unknown diameter, delineated by a plastered wall. The center of this circle contained a slab-lined pit, which Root believed was intended to hold the central support post. Two other holes were found on the circle's floor. Inside this larger circle was a smaller hole, about 3 meters in diameter, that was outlined by upright stone slabs. Additionally, 2 slab-lined pits, 1 of which contained evidence of burning, were interpreted as "signal-pits" by Root.

The importance of the dance floor in terms of the site's social and community position is hard to evaluate because there is very little hard information on it. As Smiley has suggested, this area is the same size as the so-called Great Kiva at the Shabik'eschee site in Chaco Canyon, but there is nothing comparable to it in Ridges Basin or indeed in Durango. Work initiated by Smiley will, it is hoped, reveal more about the importance of both the dance floor and the overall site complex.

In 1967, Root excavated some sites on the eastern alluvial fan of the basin (he called these the "Pasture Ruins") and also some sites on "West Animas Flats" (present-day Bodo Industrial Park, at the south end of town). Unfortunately, he did not have a lot of student help, and his recording was not up to his usual standards. Thus, we know little else about these sites, other than they had been damaged by natural erosion. Field checks of the alluvial fan in 1983 suggested that the Pasture Ruins might be 5LP 177, 179, and 243.

Root's last year of excavation on Ridges Basin was in 1969, and he was back to his normal standards of excavation and recording, despite poor health (in particular, a chronic back problem). The "East Divide Project" concentrated on a pithouse complex at the north end of the basin. The site is now called 5LP 236, but to Root, it was known as the "Hoodoo Ruin" after he had been trapped in the pithouse by a collapsed wall.

The pithouse was just over 7 meters in diameter and almost 2.5 meters deep. A bench ran the full circumference of the structure, and in it were 7 posts. The floor and lower walls were plastered, and 2 ventilator shafts were identified. A roomblock of 10 rooms lay to the northwest of the pithouse. A tree-ring date of A.D. 721 was taken from material from the complex. Unfortunately, Root never completed the artifact inventory of this site.

In 1967, John Ives excavated a large pithouse complex, now called 5LP 238, that was located on a bench behind the Bodo ranch house. The first pithouse in the complex had been destroyed by fire. The fire must have spread rapidly because many artifacts were left on the floor of the pithouse or fell into the collapsed ventilator shaft. On the floor were the remains of basketry and sleeping mats, yucca fiber, and plant remains that included amaranth seeds, corn kernels, and fragmented cobs. Three burials were found in the area.

In 1968, Ives excavated a site on the eastern alluvial fan, the major structural component of which was an east-west-oriented roomblock. Again, the fire that had destroyed the site apparently spread very quickly, since the room's contents had been left where they were. These consisted of 14 whole grayware pots. Adjacent to this roomblock, forming an el to its southwest corner, was a very poorly preserved roomblock. Across the arroyo to the north of this site, Ives also excavated another roomblock structure, again without a pithouse.

Site 5LP 630, excavated by Philip Duke and Jamie Karlson, features an unburned pithouse, a burned roomblock, and a shallow midden. The pithouse is a subrectangular structure, approximately 5 meters in diameter with a floor about 1.5 meters below the present land surface. In the center of the floor of the pithouse is a roughly circular hearth, 90 centimeters in diameter and 18 centimeters deep. Although not slab lined, it is well defined by a heavily oxidized rim around most of its circumference. This was archeomagnetically dated to about A.D. 775. In the southwest quadrant of the pithouse, approximately 20 centimeters above the floor, a partial human skeleton was recovered. Two ceramic bowls were associated with the skeleton. Human remains were located in the center of the pithouse fill as well.

To the northeast of the pithouse, a heavily burned roomblock about 5 meters by 2 meters in size was uncovered. It was impossible to distinguish any individual rooms because the structure was seriously burned and compacted. Under the roomblock was a small hearth 50 centimeters in diameter. The hearth was partially slab lined and rock filled. To the northwest of the roomblock lay a small area of heavily compacted soil approximately 2 meters by 1.5 meters in size, perhaps the remains of an activity area. A small and shallow midden area, defined by surface scatters of pottery and lithic debitage, was located to the west of the pithouse. The major features of the 5LP 242 site had previously been excavated by Ives. The area opened up by the 1981 field school lay to the west and downslope of his excavations, and it contained surface artifacts.

The 1982 field school excavations found no pithouse at 5LP 593, the major site tested that year, but the remains of a wall footing were recovered. Two storage cists, 1 of them slab lined, were also recovered. Two sites, 5LP 491 and 5LP 493, were test excavated, but neither of them revealed any subsurface features.

In 1985 and 1986, Steve Fuller, working for CASA (an archaeological consulting firm located in Cortez), excavated 11 of the sites found in Bodo Canyon, including portions of 5LP 236, which Homer Root had excavated in 1969. Fuller's work was funded by the Department of Energy, as the sites were to be affected by the relocation of the radioactive tailings pile at the south end of Durango. Two of the sites had Basketmaker II components (A.D. 200–300), and these were interpreted as shallow pithouses occupied throughout the year. Four sites were single pithouse and roomblock units dating to the Basketmaker III–Pueblo I transition; the others were nonhabitation features of the same period. These sites were expertly analyzed by Fuller and his associates, and the results of their work are found in a first-class monograph published by the Department of Energy. This work is significant because it shows the level of analytical sophistication that Durango archaeology must have if the city's past is to be fully understood.

BLUE MESA

In the 1930s, Harold Gladwin recorded a large cluster of pithouses dated to the Basketmaker III period. In his book, *A History of the Ancient Southwest*, he described the cluster as

> one of the largest Basketmaker III settlements in the area. The surface indications show four long rows of continuous rooms, stretched across the mesa, each row consisting of a double line of rectangular rooms, vaguely outlined by mounds of dirt and stones. Some of the rooms were large, some small, and some were undoubtedly used for storage, even though they were built as integral parts of the house blocks. In the open spaces between the rows of rooms there were depressions and mounds,

more or less circular, which appear to have been the ruins of large single subterranean structures, and there was a scattered group of such buildings at the southern end of the mesa. All told, the total of rooms and houses must have run to several hundred units.

Gladwin excavated at least 1 of the pithouse depressions. It was a subrectangular structure, 35 feet across by 5 feet deep. A bench 2 feet wide circled the entire structure. It contained 4 postholes, a ventilator shaft, and wing walls 18 inches high.

Site 5LP 378, excavated by Linda Honeycutt and Jerry Fetterman, had originally been located by Barry Hibbetts, a Fort Lewis College student working with John Ives. It was described by him as 2 pithouse depressions and 3 mounds. The pithouse depressions had probably been destroyed by the road that was built after Hibbetts's survey, but Honeycutt and Fetterman's crew successfully located and excavated the mounds. They unearthed the remains of 3 individual rooms, all of them oriented on a northeast-southwest axis. A tree-ring date of A.D. 782 was taken from the site.

Site 5LP 379 comprised a rubble mound, a shallow midden, and at least 1 pithouse. The pithouse had a diameter of 5 meters and an average depth of 2 meters. Four support postholes, lined with river cobbles, were recovered, and a ventilator shaft was built into the southeast side of the structure. A single rectangular room was also excavated. A tree-ring date of A.D. 831 (with a possible roof remodeling date of A.D. 839) makes this site the latest such site in the Animas valley.

Site 5LP 1380, excavated by Philip Duke in 1983, was about 4 meters in diameter and 2 meters deep. A ventilator shaft was built into the southeastern portion of the pithouse, and there was a centrally located firepit and the remains of plastering extending a little way up the wall. Associated with the pithouse were a poorly defined roomblock and 2 stone-lined cists. No timber was available for tree-ring dating, but ash from the hearth was radiocarbon-dated to A.D. 620.

BODO INDUSTRIAL PARK

Site 5LP 115, excavated by Susan Riches, was a pithouse just under 5 meters in diameter, containing 4 postholes and a partial bench.

A.2 A classic Basketmaker III water jar, or *olla*, from 5LP 119. Note the narrow neck and the side handles used to facilitate carrying it or hanging it from a roof. Courtesy, Department of Anthropology, Fort Lewis College.

In association with it were at least 3 adobe rooms. This structure then burned, and a new occupation of the pithouse was initiated. Both occupations were dated to the late eighth century (based on tree-ring samples and ceramics).

Site 5LP 119 was also excavated by Riches. The pithouse measured about 7 meters in diameter and had a full bench, wing walls, and a ventilator shaft. A later firepit and a dog burial were found in the fill of the depression, as well as some typical Basketmaker pottery that could be reconstructed into virtually whole vessels (Figures A.2 and A.3). Northeast of the pithouse, a roomblock had been badly vandalized by pothunters. The ceramic data and architectural style suggest that the site was transitional between the Basketmaker III and Pueblo I periods. Two occupations were identified during excavation within the pit structure—the pit structure itself and a temporary reoccupation of the pit structure after abandonment. A hearth feature was exca-

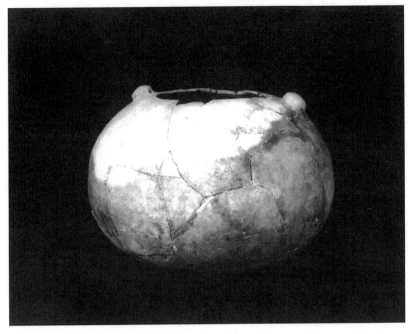

A.3 A typical Basketmaker III general-purpose storage vessel from 5LP 119. Note the lugs on the neck. Courtesy, Department of Anthropology, Fort Lewis College.

vated from the fill above the roof fall. A roomblock area was evident approximately 10 meters northwest of the pit structure and contained ceramics, flaked lithics, human bone fragments, sandstone slabs, and depressions. This area was badly vandalized by pothunters. Due to lack of time and construction scheduling, the roomblock area was not excavated.

Site 5LP 138, originally designated as 5LP 117, is a large Basketmaker III–Pueblo I habitation site. Salvage excavations were conducted by Fort Lewis College in the late 1970s in anticipation of impending construction, which ultimately did not take place. A large, deep pit structure, along with a series of 3 contiguous sandstone slab rooms northwest of the pit structure and 2 to 3 rooms north of the pit structure, were the focus of these early investigations. Human remains representing at least 5 individuals were recovered during the excavations. One recovered artifact was a virtually unbroken cooking vessel (Figure A.4).

A.4 Basketmaker III cooking vessel from 5LP 117. Mottling on its surface was caused by both a poor firing atmosphere and exposure to a fire during use. Courtesy, Department of Anthropology, Fort Lewis College.

Most recently, excavations at site 5LP 138 uncovered a large, rectangular portion of the site south of the pit structure in the remaining portions of the midden. A total area of 120 square meters was subjected to either shovel stripping or complete excavation. These excavations increased the artifact count of the site, but the only features that were recognized was a large, basin-shaped storage cist and a single posthole.

Site 5LP 126 is located at the southeast corner of Turner Drive and La Posta Road (County Road 213). This site has been cut along its eastern edge by La Posta Road and by Turner Drive to the north. A small but dense artifact scatter along the eastern margin adjacent to La Posta Road was identified as a midden deposit. It is very possible that the habitation units were removed by the construction of Turner Drive.

A.5 Pit structure 1, 5LP 425, from the 1994 excavations by Mona Charles. Courtesy, Mona Charles.

Site 5LP 425 was partially excavated by Fort Lewis College in 1980. It is a Basketmaker III–Pueblo I habitation site consisting of at least 3 pit structures and several slab-lined surface features. The field school excavated a single pitstructure, a sandstone slab work area with several surface hearths, and a small roomblock north of the pit structure. A reoccupation of the pit structure was indicated by a postabandonment hearth above the roof fall. Neither the pit structure nor the roomblock was burned.

Mona Charles conducted further excavations at 5LP 425 in the fall of 1994. Her crew excavated a small midden area, a large slab-lined cist, and 2 pit structures. One pit structure was located adjacent to the pit structure excavated by Fort Lewis College, and a second appeared in a backhoe trench across a large arroyo from the other 2 pit structures in an area that Fort Lewis students had examined and determined to consist of shallow sheet-midden deposits. Neither of the pit structures was burned; instead, both appeared to have been casually abandoned. The pit structure adjacent to the Fort Lewis pit structure measured about 6 meters in diameter and was just over 2 meters deep (Figure A.5). It was square to round in shape with a three-quarter bench. Floor features included a ventilator shaft, a central hearth, 3 main post support holes, 2 sipapus, and 5 floor storage features. A fourth main support post is assumed, but it was not located. The pervasive rodent and root disturbance at this site hampered accurate feature identification. The central hearth was almost completely destroyed by rodent burrows, and so little of the feature remained that an archaeomagnetic sample could not be taken.

A second pit structure was located in a backhoe trench across the drainage and 30 meters east of the main site area. It did not possess a bench feature, and the floor measurements almost mirrored those of the previous pit structure. Shallower than the other pit structure, this pit structure differed from most excavated in the Bodo area in that it was partially filled with trash. A relatively dense trash fill began about 1 meter above the floor and continued to the contact with the floor. The pit structure did not possess a bench, and the remains of a wing wall (or walls) were only hinted at. A ventilator shaft was excavated, but there was no evidence of a deflector. Thirty-three floor features were excavated with the pit structure. These include 2 hearths, 2 wall niches, 4 main support postholes, 15 small postholes, 8 storage features, and an upright metate that was probably once part of the wing wall. A possible explanation for the small postholes included depressions made in the surface from resting weaving looms. Similar features at nearby sites were interpreted by archaeologist John Gooding as the remains of short partition wall storage features. Up to 3 subtle floor remodelings were present in the area south of the northern hearth. The last remodeling effort successfully covered the southern hearth, the earlier of the 2 hearths. Among other artifacts recovered from the fill were the remains of at least 8 dogs.

An unusual sub-rounded, stone-lined cist was excavated at the site. This feature measured 2.4 meters by 2.4 meters and was about 80 centimeters deep. The feature was constructed of large sandstone slabs that lined both the sides and the bottom of the feature.

Two more sites (5LP 110 and 111) were excavated in 1976 by John Gooding. Site 5LP 110 was a sub-rectangular pithouse approximately 6 meters in diameter. A bench ran around about three-quarters of the pithouse. The floor was plastered. Log debris was tree-ring-dated to A.D. 752 to 776. Work areas to the west of the

A.6 Trough metate and two-handed mano from 5LP 135. Courtesy, Department of Anthropology, Fort Lewis College.

roomblock were dated to A.D. 675. North and east of the pithouse, Gooding recovered a number of skeletons, 1 of which had an *olivella* (a marine mollusk) bracelet on its wrist.

Site 5LP 111 consisted of 2 subterranean features. The first was a small pit structure 2.5 meters in diameter. The second was a larger pithouse, 6 meters in diameter with a three-quarters bench. The hearth was dated by archeomagnetism to A.D. 720.

Between 1994 and 1996, Steve Fuller surveyed 45 acres of land south of Durango as part of an annexation project related to the highways there. Fuller found 10 sites. These included segments of the Denver and Rio Grande Railroad grade, a Historic period homestead that had been occupied until the 1970s, a twentieth-century irrigation ditch, and 6 Ancestral Pueblo sites. Although 4 of these were heavily disturbed, the other 2 still appear to have structures intact.

COLLEGE MESA AND THE SOUTH END OF TOWN

Ignacio 12:23 is a pithouse and roomblock complex at the north end of the mesa excavated by Flora in 1935. In 1936, Helen Sloan

Daniels conducted more intensive investigations in this area. One burial was recovered. The tree-ring dates are ambiguous, placing the site anywhere between A.D. 430 and 670. Few other data are available.

Site 5LP 135 is a Basketmaker III pithouse, originally excavated by Susan Riches in 1976 and 1977; it is approximately 4 meters in diameter and 2 meters deep. It contained plastered walls, a firepit, 4 postholes, a ventilator shaft, wing walls, and 2 recessed wall cists. Of interest was the fact that the beams had been removed from the postholes and that the holes were filled with sand and then capped with plaster. A noncutting tree-ring date of A.D. 586 was obtained from this site. Figure A.6 shows a mano and metate recovered from the site. In 1998, Mona Charles and the Fort Lewis College field school reexcavated the site to reevaluate its potential for yielding further information. Charles and her students also completed a full, interpretive site report for 5LP 135.

CRESTVIEW

In 1938, Helen Sloan Daniels excavated a series of sites in what was then called Griffiths Heights, on the western edge of town. One site, Ignacio 12:1, had first been trenched by Zeke Flora in 1934 for tree-ring specimens, and in fact this was the first site to provide datable wood in Durango (from the early part of the seventh century). Daniels's excavations were supervised by Frank Lee, a graduate of Durango High School and a sophomore at the University of Colorado. They revealed an oval pithouse 23 feet (east-west) by 19 feet (north-south), with an average depth of 7 feet. A bench 2 feet wide circled the whole structure. The walls and floor still were plastered, and architectural features included a fire hearth, a ventilator shaft in the south wall, a deflector slab, and a wall niche in the southwest corner. Charred corn remains were found.

Ignacio 12:58 was a benched pithouse with surface structures about which little is known. The construction date may have been in the late seventh century. Ignacio 12:59 was described by Daniels in her final report in this way: "It had been our hope to uncover a roof of a surface dwelling which had fallen flat and this was found at 12:59. The main support timbers found at the corners were salvaged for dating purposes. Small cross timbers were stretched between the main posts and uniform timbers laid parallel across them. It was probably built some time after A.D. 660."

Ignacio 12:4 was trenched by Flora in the mid-1930s and is located on Griffiths Heights (i.e., Crestview), at the north end in the vicinity of Dry Creek. No structures were described at the site. Ambiguous tree-ring dates place the site somewhere between A.D. 450 and 650.

Ignacio 12:10 is in the same general vicinity as Ignacio 12:4. It was a circular pithouse with a full bench. There is some indication that the pithouse was built into an existing site. Tree-ring dates place construction some time in the early seventh century.

MISCELLANEOUS SITES

In 1936, Daniels turned her attention to Ignacio 12:18. Her description of the site's location is as follows: "It is located at the southern end of Folsom's Mesa, a low bluff of glacial gravel, on the east side of the Animas River where Junction Creek empties into the Animas. It is reached by the highway which continues the northern end of Third Avenue. This site, which is now city property, was chosen because the excavations for the city gravel pit had reached the southern brink of this ruin."

The site had already been damaged by gravel extraction work before Daniels was able to start her excavations, but it was still possible to discern the outline of a "horseshoe-shaped ridge [roomblock] which surrounded the central depression." Numerous burials, sherds, stone tools, and datable wood were removed. The site was destroyed completely by the city's gravel workings in 1938.

Ignacio 12:27 is about 2 miles south of town on the east bank of the Animas (close to where Sawmill Road is today). The site was a burned pithouse, 34 feet by 32 feet, with a floor about 8 feet below the surface. A bench 3.5 feet high ringed the structure. The walls and floor were plastered, and the pithouse contained 4 postholes, a hearth, a ventilator shaft, and wing walls made of stone and adobe. The pithouse was surrounded by a block of rooms. The fire that destroyed the site gave Flora the opportunity to recover woven baskets, ears of corn, charred beans, pine needles, and sagebrush stems. Over 40 burials were recovered, as well as numerous ceramic vessels, manos, and metates. Flora dated its construction to about A.D. 630. A review of the tree-ring dates by Jeffrey Dean of the Laboratory of Tree-Ring Research at the University of Arizona indicated that either it was built in A.D. 630, with a later reconstruction or use in the eighth century, or that the house was first built in the eighth century, using older timber.

Helen Sloan Daniels also recovered the remains of human burials in the 3500 block of Main Avenue in 1955. Unfortunately, the site had already been virtually destroyed. Other isolated finds are located within the city limits, and nearly all of them have been found by nonprofessionals.

Site 5LP 1859 was excavated by the Fort Lewis College field school in 1985 under the direction of Philip Duke. Most of the pithouse had been destroyed by the construction of a modern house. The floor was about 1.25 meters below the present ground surface, and it appeared to have been remodeled several times. It contained a hearth, 40 centimeters in diameter and 25 centimeters deep, and also a shallow circular pit 55 centimeters wide and 15 centimeters deep. Ceramic jars containing corn kernels were found in the burned roof material, and it is possible that these pots had been hanging from the pithouse's roof prior to the burning that destroyed it. A small piece of wood from the floor of the structure was radiocarbon-dated to about A.D. 450.

During the city's expansion after the end of the World War II, construction and other activities regularly uncovered archaeological remains, recorded by the *Durango Herald*. The following is a sampling of what was uncovered.

At the corner of West 3rd Avenue and 24th Street, 6 to 8 skeletons, 6 to 7 pots, a stone hammer, 2 metates, and a "medicine man's kit" were found. In 1950, Abe Beltram found a bowl and a decomposed skeleton while digging 1 of the piers for the Mason School. Four skeletons and associated pottery were found in the yard of 854 5th Street. In 1960, at least 4 skeletons and 6 bowls were recovered from the site of Saint Paul's Lutheran Church on Junction Creek Road. Later, the tally rose to 9 skeletons, as well as projectile points, a stone axe, and more pottery. In 1961, in the yard of the home at 1039 5th Avenue owned by Ed Canterbury, a disintegrating skeleton, a ceramic pitcher, and a bowl were found.

Suggested Readings

GENERAL ARCHAEOLOGY

Archaeology: Theories, Methods, and Practice, by Colin Renfrew and
   Paul Bahn (2d ed., London: Thames and Hudson, 1996)
   Probably the best synthesis available on how modern archaeology is conducted. All the major theoretical stances are described
   in full, together with all the different methods and techniques
   used by modern archaeologists.

Discovering Our Past, by Wendy Ashmore and Robert Shearer (2d ed.,
   Mountain View, Calif.: Mayfield Publishing, 1998)
   A college textbook that provides a brief and clearly written
   review of the science of archaeology.

The Collins Dictionary of Archaeology, edited by Paul Bahn (Edinburgh:
   Collins, 1992)
   The most complete and up-to-date dictionary of world archaeology, listing not only the major sites but also all the terms and
   concepts used by archaeologists.

NORTH AMERICAN ARCHAEOLOGY

Ancient North America, by Brian Fagan (2d ed., London: Thames and
   Hudson, 1995)
   A comprehensive review of the prehistory of the continent,
   with lavish illustrations and a clear, easy-to-read text.

FOUR CORNERS ARCHAEOLOGY

The Archaeology of Colorado, by Steve Cassells (rev. ed., Boulder: Johnson Books, 1997)

The best single introduction to the state's prehistory, this well-illustrated and comprehensive book is specifically written for the general public.

Archaeology of the Eastern Ute: A Symposium, edited by Paul Nickens (Denver: Colorado Council of Professional Archaeologists, 1988)

Written for the professional, this volume reports on a conference symposium that attempted to synthesize current archaeological knowledge on the Ute.

Enemy Ancestors, by Gary Matlock and Scott Warren (1st ed., Flagstaff, Ariz.: Northland Press, 1987; now out of print but still available in some bookstores)

A wonderful introduction to the Anasazi, with beautiful photographs and a clear and detailed text.

Legacy on Stone: Rock Art of the Colorado Plateau and Four Corners Region, by Sally Cole (Boulder: Johnson Books, 1990)

The definitive analysis of Four Corners rock art.

The Four Corners Anasazi, by Rose Houck (Durango, Colo.: San Juan National Forest Association, 1994)

A nontechnical overview of the region's archaeology written specifically for the layperson.

Mesa Verde National Park: Shadows of the Centuries, by Duane Smith (Lawrence: University Press of Kansas, 1988)

A detailed and well-researched book on the history of the nation's first archaeological national park.

Archaeology of the Southwest, by Linda Cordell (2d ed., San Diego, Calif.: Academic Press, 1997)

Although written for the professional, this book, with its clarity of prose, is an excellent resource for the layperson interested in the details of Southwest archaeology.

Ancient Pueblo Peoples, by Linda Cordell (Washington, D.C.: Smithsonian Books, 1995)

A clearly written and well-illustrated review of Southwest archaeology.

Anasazi Ruins of the Southwest in Color, by Arthur Rohn and William Ferguson (1st ed., Albuquerque: University of New Mexico Press, 1986)

A superb collection of aerial photographs of the most important sites in the Four Corners region, accompanied by an excellent and informative text.

The State of Colorado Archaeology, edited by Philip Duke and Gary Matlock (Denver: Colorado Archaeology Society, 1992)

A collection of articles by amateur and professional archaeologists on various aspects of Colorado archaeology.

The Western San Juan Mountains, edited by Rob Blair (Niwot: University Press of Colorado, Fort Lewis College Foundation, 1996)

A collection of essays for the public describing the human and natural history of the mountains north of Durango.

DURANGO ARCHAEOLOGY AND HISTORY

Animas–La Plata Archaeological Project Research Papers, edited by Francis E. Smiley (Bureau of Reclamation, 1995)

A series of reports on various topics concerning Ridges Basin archaeology. These reports were generated by federal preservation requirements; although produced primarily for the professional, they are well written and clear enough for the nonprofessional to understand.

Archaeological Investigations in the Bodo Canyon Area, La Plata County, Colorado, by Steven Fuller (Albuquerque, N. Mex.: Jacobs Engineering Group, 1988)

A technical report written for the professional and one of the most comprehensive studies of Durango archaeology.

The Cultural Resources of Ridges Basin and Upper Wildcat Canyon, by Joseph Winter, W. E. Reynolds, and J. Ware (Durango: Bureau of Reclamation, 1981)

A technical report that describes the results of the comprehensive survey of Ridges Basin.

Fort Lewis College Archaeological Investigations in Ridges Basin, Southwest Colorado: 1965–1982, by Philip Duke (Occasional Paper 4, Center of Southwest Studies, Fort Lewis College, 1985)

113

A technical report that documents the various archaeological studies done in Ridges Basin since Homer Root's work in the 1960s.

The Durango South Project, by John Gooding (Anthropological Papers of the University of Arizona 34, 1980)

A report of salvage excavations south of Durango.

Prehistory in Peril, by Florence Lister (Niwot: University Press of Colorado, 1997)

A history of archaeological investigations at the Falls Creek Rock Shelters, concentrating on Zeke Flora's positive and negative impact on Durango archaeology.

Rocky Mountain Boom Town, by Duane Smith (1st ed., Albuquerque: University of New Mexico Press, 1980)

The standard and enduring history of Durango.

Tree-Ring Dates From Colorado W—Durango Area, by Jeffrey S. Dean (Tucson: Laboratory of Tree-Ring Research, University of Arizona, 1975)

A technical report on the hundreds of tree-ring dates from Durango-area sites, it is probably of most use to professionals.

The Durango Public Library Museum Project, by Helen Sloan Daniels (Durango, Colo.: Durango Public Library, 1940)

Prepared by Daniels as part of her Durango Library Project, this report provides a fascinating glimpse into the work of this amateur archaeologist.

Sherds and Points

A "journal" produced in 1940 and 1941 by Zeke Flora and Helen Sloan Daniels, now in the collection of the Center of Southwest Studies, Fort Lewis College. Some interesting articles on Durango sites are included.

Index

Amundsen, Ted, 67
Anasazi (Ancestral Pueblo), 2, 4, 15, 26, 36, 40–42, 67, 75, 88–91
Ancestral Pueblo. *See* Anasazi
Animas City, 53
Animas–La Plata Project, 36, 38
Animas Museum, 82
Archaeology, defined 3–6; culture history, 4, 59; historical, 17; postprocessualism, 6, 60; processualism, 6, 59–60; and Native Americans, 7
Archaic Period, 13–14, 25–26, 42
Archeomagnetic Dating, 5–6

Ballantine Family, 81, 86
Basketmaker Period, 15, 26–29, 33, 35–38, 40, 42–44, 50, 64, 73, 87, 90, 93–95, 100, 102–103, 105, 108
Bering Land Bridge, 10–11
Berry, Michael, 43
Biggs, Bill, 50
Binford, Lewis, 59
Black Mountain Site, 23
Blue Mesa, 28, 38, 100–101
Bodo Canyon, 25, 37, 100
Bodo Industrial Park, 28, 39, 101–107
Braandsma, Cheryle, 83

Bradley, Bruce, 25
Brockway, Charles, 83
Burgh, Robert, 32–33

Camp, Estell, 66
Carlson, Roy, 35, 94
Chaco Canyon, 1, 8, 98
Chandler, Susan, 38
Charles, Mona, 39, 46, 81, 95, 105–106, 108
Children's Museum of Durango, 82
Clovis Culture, 12, 23–25
Cole, Sally, 94
College Mesa, 28, 39–40
Colorado Federated Women's Club, 66
Cotton, Ernie, 34
Crestview, 22, 28, 40–41, 108–109

Daniels, Helen Sloan, 2, 32, 35, 40, 55, 70–72, 82, 107–110
Darkmold Site, 35, 95–96
Dating Techniques, 4–6
Dean, Jeffrey, 22, 109
Deloria, Jr., Vine, 89
Dold, Mark, 95
Dominguez-Escalante Expedition, 61–62